CW01080571

THE

AMAZING

ARCHIE

Copyright © 2022 by Anthony Conrad (words and interior illustrations).

All rights reserved.

No portion of this book may be reproduced in any form without written permission from the publisher or author.

Cover illustration © Martina Delloca

ISBN: 9798367239362

To Mum & Dad, Stephanie and Dee

CHAPTER 1

CHLOE MORAN WAS SURE that if she did not find out what was in the box within the next five minutes, her twelve-year-old brain would suffer some sort of irreparable meltdown.

Her mum, Edith, did not seem aware of this possibility. She sat in a luxurious armchair and drummed her slim fingers on the side of the only remaining unopened box from their recent move.

'Mum, what's inside?' Chloe asked.

Edith drummed quicker and louder.

'Mum?' Chloe whined, moving closer.

The box was a little under Chloe's height. Thick brown tape sealed the flaps, and one side read, 'Grunters Chicken Soup.' Edith snapped out of her semi-trance and turned to her petite, ever-curious daughter.

'It's not really chicken soup, is it?' Chloe asked, playing with her shoulder-length brown hair.

Edith let out a slow breath. 'Shall we watch the documentary that's about to come on?'

This wasn't the response Chloe had been expecting. 'Why would I want to watch a documentary?'

'Because after we've watched it, I'll show you what's in the box.'

If there was any logic to this sentence, Chloe failed to see it.

'Just trust me,' Edith said.

'Can't you just tell me now?'

Edith gave a slight smile. 'Let's put it another way. You sit down with me and watch this TV programme, and then we'll open the box together, or we don't, and the contents stay secret for all time. What do you think?'

'Sounds a bit unfair,' Chloe said, plonking herself on the sofa.

'Life's unfair.'

'Dad used to say that.'

Edith's smile tightened. 'We separated. He's not dead.'

Chloe made a huffing noise but made no further complaint. Her mum was of a somewhat nervous disposition these days, and she didn't want to make things worse.

Edith switched on a large TV and began to flick through the channels.

'Does George have to watch?' Chloe asked. Her brother George was two years older than her and seldom left his bedroom.

'No, just the two of us, I think. Won't that be nice?'

'I guess,' Chloe said. She stretched her legs out and noticed her socks were uneven. She pulled the left one up to match the right. 'Okay, we can watch it.'

'You're so kind.'

The title read, 'The Amazing Archie, a sixtieth-anniversary special.' Underneath the title, what looked like a well-dressed brown bear leaned against a lamppost with his arms crossed. He had a mischievous grin and looked unusually lifelike.

Chloe recoiled in horror. 'Mum, it's in black-and-white!'

'Only the old bits. It won't kill you.'

Chloe let out a garbled cry and grabbed her throat. Her head slumped onto her shoulder, and her tongue hung out of the corner of her mouth. With her dying breath, she whispered, 'Tell my friends—that never call—that I forgive them...' and then she was gone.

'Don't be so dramatic,' Edith said. 'Once upon a time, everything was in black and white. Early films didn't even have sound.'

Chloe lifted her head. 'That was ages and ages ago, when you were little.'

Edith frowned. 'I'm only thirty-five, thank you very much.'

'And it's about a toy bear. I'm not a baby!'

'I think you're being slightly unfair. It's a very charismatic bear and not at all cute.'

Chloe crossed her arms in disgust and decided she would not enjoy it, no matter what.

A portly presenter with a kind face and an ugly striped jumper strolled across the set and sunk into a comfortable armchair. The screen changed to colour, and to Chloe's surprise, the man's jumper looked even worse. He addressed the camera.

'We're here today to celebrate one of children's most loved characters. Unbelievably, it is sixty years today since his first TV appearance. I am, of course, talking about Archie. Or to give him his full title, *The Amazing Archie*. Over the next hour, we'll speak to some of his fans and a few of the surviving team responsible for the show. We'll also hear some theories about Archie's disappearance.'

Chloe noticed that at that point, her mum chose to look at the ceiling, which was slightly odd, given her insistence that they watch together.

'But first, and especially for those of you who have not yet met Archie, let's see him in action with the first-ever episode, *Cave In*.'

'Not enjoying it so far,' Chloe complained.

'Give it a chance,' Edith replied.

The screen faded to a picturesque black-and-white landscape. On the brow of a hill, the star of the show, Archie, sneaked through a line of trees. He had a pronounced muzzle, his head crowned with tufty forward-pointing hair, and he had bushy eyebrows. A splash of white fur ran from his throat to his chest and poked through his partially open shirt. He wore striped trousers and dark braces to keep them up.

The stop motion style was a little jerky, but Chloe knew that animating a bear was probably quite challenging, and it was really old, so she'd make allowances.

As Archie crept across the landscape, the camera panned down the hill toward a family picnic. A woman lay on a blanket near a solitary tree, an attractive wooden picnic basket at her side, and a summer hat rested on her face. Beside her, a small boy—aged about five or six—ran a toy car along a blanket and made engine noises.

In the distance, a mining colliery sat silhouetted against rolling hills. It was a wooden cut-out painted black, but it looked quite real.

Archie left the cover of trees and crept towards the picnic. The woman and her young son were oblivious. The boy decided the car was now a plane and whizzed it through the air.

Archie stopped at the tree beside them and waited for the boy to look away. He tiptoed the last few metres and silently picked up the picnic basket from the blanket.

The boy turned and gasped.

Archie put a paw to his mouth. 'Sssshhhh.'

The boy watched in amazement as Archie tiptoed away with the basket.

Chloe's jaw dropped. 'Mum, he stole their picnic!'

'I know. I was watching.'

Chloe crossed her arms and glared at the TV.

The young boy turned to his mother. 'Mum!' When she didn't answer, he shook her shoulder.

She stirred. 'What, Jake?'

'A bear!'

'What?'

'A bear took the picnic!'

'Don't be silly. We don't have bears here.' She removed the hat from her face and studied the blanket. 'Where's the picnic?'

'I told you, a bear took it!' Jake pointed into the distance.

She stood and held a hand to her eyebrows as she tried to make out the small shape scampering towards the trees. 'I can't see—it's probably a child. It's not a bear!'

Jake's shoulders slumped. 'It *was* a bear!'

'Don't tell stories.' His mum set off in pursuit of the thief. 'Hello! I say, excuse me!' The gap increased. 'Come back, and maybe I won't tell your parents!' She shifted into a lumbering run.

Archie turned and saw the woman gaining ground, so he sped up.

Jake's lower lip trembled. 'Mum, come back!' He got to his feet and ran after her.

Archie made it to the tree line, and then a slight rumble made him stop. He looked around, then down at his feet. The ground appeared to be moving.

There was a loud CRACKKKKKKKK!

The boy screamed as he slid down a collapsing shelf of earth, arms flailing for something to halt his fall but finding only air.

The woman twisted around and watched the earth swallow her son. 'Jake!' she screamed and, breathing heavily, she ran back down the hill. She fell to her knees at the chasm. 'Jake! Can you hear me? Answer Mummy.'

The hole in the earth was too narrow for her frame—for most human frames. She turned towards the colliery. 'Help! Please, anyone...'

Turning back, she dug at the earth. But it was hopeless. 'Jake, honey, please answer me.'

Chloe watched intently, caught up in the drama despite herself. It was remarkably tense for an old show.

Archie's eyes were wide with terror, flicking between the mother and the hole that had swallowed her son.

The distressed woman wiped soil and tears from her face. 'Don't worry, baby. I'll get help.' After a last lingering look, she ran.

Archie gazed at the safety of the woods, hesitated for a moment, and then turned and ran back towards the disaster. Halfway there, he dropped the picnic basket to the ground. Sandwiches, rolls and cake scattered across the grass. A bottle top popped off, releasing a stream of red liquid into the soil. It fizzed for a few seconds before the earth drank it up.

Archie skidded to a halt, inches from the hole. He scanned the area and then peered over the narrow opening. Its edges, ragged with torn vegetation, allowed little sunlight inside. With his large paws, he tried to widen the hole. A root came free, and he eased it from the soil until he had a good length to hold. He tested it for strength, held tight, and squeezed himself through the tight opening.

The camera angle changed to an interior shot looking up. Archie's legs dangled, black shadows against the slithers of light surrounding him. He looked for another root, but suddenly the one he was holding gave way, and he dropped.

An ominous chord sounded, causing Chloe to thrust a hand to her mouth.

Archie came to a sudden stop. The root had pulled free from the earth but remained intact. He caught his breath, found another root and continued down.

As the hole darkened, small pairs of lights pierced the dark. Archie gave them a wary glance but continued deeper.

'Jake, can you hear me?'

'Help...' came a feeble reply.

Archie scanned the void. 'Louder, please.'

The boy's strength was draining fast. 'Over... here...'

Archie looked around but couldn't see him. 'Again, please.'

Silence.

'Come on, Jake, try to make a noise. Anything you like. Surprise me.'

Twisted wooden joists were just visible in places. It was an old coal mine. 'Why me?' Archie grumbled.

A high-pitched squeal broke the silence as a colony of bats dropped from the ceiling and circled the cavern. Archie ducked and followed the noise. The small mammals regrouped in an alcove not far off. 'Bats' eyes!' he said, realising what the lights were. There was a boy-shaped silhouette beneath them.

The floor beneath him was difficult to make out—it could be a few feet below, but maybe more. Archie plucked a stone from the cave wall and dropped it. 'One... two...' The stone hit the ground before he'd finished the second number. He stared into the darkness for a moment, gulped, and then released his grip.

He hit the ground hard and buckled.

Even Chloe winced in sympathy for the bear.

The bats emitted a squeal of alarm, but after a minute, silence returned, and Archie staggered upright.

There was a rustle of motion at the entrance to the cave. 'Jake, can you hear us?' someone called.

Archie's head snapped towards the voice. He gritted his teeth and pressed on down the slope towards the boy.

More voices joined the first, including the sobs of the boy's mother. Archie shook his head, seemingly conflicted over whether to reveal himself. Finally, he shouted back. 'Don't worry, I see him.'

'Who are you?' someone above shouted.

'Name's Archie.'

'How did you get in there?'

'You'll see,' Archie muttered, and he continued deeper. The bats took flight, skimming his head as he continued to the cave wall. He felt around and found a foot, and attached to that, a whole boy.

Someone lowered a torch on a piece of rope. As it came down, it spun around, casting a disc of light around the cave walls.

Archie checked the boy over. His breathing was shallow, but there was no sign of serious injury, just a nasty gash across his forehead.

'How are you doing?' Archie asked.

Jake moaned something.

'Save your energy. I'm going to get you out.'

The boy looked at him with scared eyes but managed a slight nod.

Archie took the boy gently under the arms, carefully dragged him towards the entrance, and then set him down on the ground. He grabbed the torch, which was still hanging from the length of rope, looked up nervously towards the growing number of voices, and then shone it around the cave. The cone of light illuminated a collapsed tunnel, which Archie studied carefully.

Chloe perched on the edge of the sofa. 'Archie doesn't want anyone to see him, does he?'

'Would you, if you were a talking bear?' Edith asked.

'No way!'

A voice called down into the cavern. 'What's happening?'

Archie scanned every dark corner but couldn't see an alternative exit. 'We're below you,' he shouted back.

'Can you move him?'

'He just has a few cuts and bruises, as far as I can tell.'

'Tie the rope around him, under his arms. We've got a rope ladder coming as well.'

Archie exhaled slowly. 'Okay.'

He wrapped the rope around the boy as instructed before tying it off. Above, a motorbike approached at speed, followed by a squeal of breaks, silence and then a rustle of movement.

'Mind your head!' someone shouted.

Archie stepped back as a rope ladder unravelled in front of him. He looked back at the collapsed tunnel and then up at the slithers of light above. Now and then, the light dimmed as someone leaned over the hole.

With a shake of his head, he climbed the ladder, carrying the little boy as best he could. 'Pull!'

The crowd pulled, and the boy inched upwards. With each pull, Archie clambered up another rung.

Jake regained a little strength when he heard voices above. As he neared the opening, he stretched two small arms upwards, and his grateful mother plucked him from the hole. The crowd gave a tremendous cheer.

Archie climbed the last few rungs and wrestled his body through the narrow opening into the sunlight. He staggered to his feet, shielding his eyes with a paw.

The boy's mum looked at him with a mixture of awe and anger. Finally, she gave Archie a slight nod and carried her son away. A few feet away, the boy mumbled, 'I told you there was a bear.'

The jubilant crowd became silent, unsure of what they were seeing.

Archie took his paw away from his eyes. 'Afternoon.'

There were blank looks. Some of the crowd nervously reached for family or friends and pulled them closer.

'Have I got something on my face?' Archie asked, pretending to check his face for food. He grinned nervously.

Whispered conversation spread through the crowd.

Archie looked towards the tree line. 'Well, it's been a pleasure. I'll be on my way now.'

An important-looking man edged forward. 'I don't know who or what you are, but thank you.' He looked to the crowd. 'We'd love to show our appreciation. Maybe some drinks and nibbles... if you're interested?'

'It's fine,' Archie said. 'I was, err... in the area.'

'You're sure?'

Archie looked around. 'Regrettably, I have plans.'

'You don't need to worry about that lot,' the man said, gesturing at the crowd. 'You're safe.' He turned back. 'Isn't he?'

A few of the crowd nodded, but most continued to stare at Archie in awe as they struggled with the reality of a talking bear.

'You're one of us now.'

Another voice in the crowd shouted. 'One of us!'

And then another. 'One of us!'

And then everyone began to chant. 'One of us! One of us! One of us!'

Archie turned to the camera and gave a large cheesy grin.

Chloe clapped. 'Yay! I wonder what happens next?' She then remembered she hated black-and-white TV and stopped talking.

The presenter beamed. 'And there you have it, the first of Archie's many adventures. Unfortunately, Archie often got things wrong, and part of the show's success was the lessons he learnt. But he was a well-spoken bear—when he wanted to be—and could talk himself out of most scrapes. After the break, we'll go to "Heaven Can Wait", a care home favoured by creative types, where we'll talk to writer Barry Boston Boyle about the two sides to Archie's personality: Archie, occasional criminal mastermind and Archie, the bear that would risk his life to help others. We'll discuss the cost of creating him and the show. Spoiler—it wasn't cheap! And we'll look at Archie's sixty-year-long disappearance. Be right back!'

Edith hastily switched off the TV. 'Maybe we don't need to watch the whole thing. So, what did you think?'

'It was alright,' Chloe said.

'You were glued to it!'

'It was quite good for a black-and-white programme. I'm glad Archie saved the boy!'

'See, he wasn't so bad after all.'

Chloe wasn't sure. It seemed to her that if Archie hadn't stolen the picnic, the boy wouldn't have been hurt in the first place.

'I suppose it's time,' Edith said uncertainly.

'For what?'

'The box.'

'Oh yes!' Chloe's eyes brightened. She'd almost forgotten about the box.

CHAPTER 2

CHLOE WATCHED AS HER mum shoved her skinny arms into the coffee table drawer and rummaged around for scissors to open the mysterious box. She looked tired. After a challenging year, they'd moved into Mum's sister Carole's house in London. Carole was working abroad for a year for a large bank—she had no children and, according to Mum, more money than the Queen of Sheba, whoever she was. As lovely as the house was, Chloe hoped the move was temporary.

Edith found the scissors and held them up triumphantly. 'Why the serious face?'

'No reason,' Chloe said and forced a smile.

Edith slid a blade along the seal and prised the flaps open.

Chloe peered in. Screwed-up newspaper surrounded a wooden box. She scooped some aside to see what treasures lay hidden within.

'Patience,' Edith said. 'Hold the sides of the box for me, please.'

Chloe grasped the sides whilst Edith prised a wooden casket out. It looked expensive—quality oak sides with elaborate swirls and flourishes carved along the top and bottom rim of the box. Iron bars were set across a window in a hinged door.

Edith lowered the casket to the floor and turned it so the window faced her daughter. Chloe gasped, but not because she admired the workmanship. The box contained a bear, and not just any old bear. Chloe was so excited that her cheeks began to burn.

'Chloe, breathe,' Edith encouraged.

'That's Archie!'

'Yes, it is.'

'Is it the real Archie? I mean, the one that went missing?'

Edith looked a little embarrassed. She nodded.

'Wow... How do you have it?'

'My grandfather—your great grandfather—worked on the show. I don't know what happened, but there were rumours that he thought Archie was special. I think he'd want you to have him.'

'Special?'

Edith shrugged. 'Apparently.'

Chloe nibbled at her lower lip.

'I thought you'd be excited,' Edith said.

'I am! This is so cool. But that documentary said he's been missing for years.'

'You know, if he hadn't been missing, I doubt anyone would have given him a second thought.'

'He's famous, Mum,' Chloe said and looked at her mum as if she was mad.

Edith gazed into space for a moment. 'I suppose he is. Why don't we get him out, and then we'll talk?' She gave her daughter an iron key.

Chloe slid the key into the hole and gave it a turn. There was a satisfying click. She opened the door, wrapped her small arms around Archie's torso, and pulled him out. He was big, four foot maybe, and wore striped trousers, shirt, and braces, just like in the TV show. His limbs were flexible, and even his facial features moved. But he wasn't cute. The bear's rugged features set him apart from mere toys.

'He's heavy,' Chloe said.

'Metal skeleton, like Wolverine.'

Chloe heaved the bear onto her lap and ran her fingers through his fur coat, and then the strangest feeling came over her.

Archie could take it no longer. The corners of his mouth curled into a smile, and he leapt from Chloe's lap.

Chloe and Edith were completely unaware of this, as the second Archie moved, they froze like statues. It was as if time had stopped.

Archie landed on the floor and put his right paw down to prevent himself from falling on his face. 'I'm free!' he cried with delight. Then he staggered up, hopped onto the coffee table, wobbled a bit, jumped down and ran into a display cabinet, knocking over a delightful silver elephant figurine. Archie steadied himself, then charged from the room and ran upstairs.

He burst into a modern bathroom—white suite, grey slate tiles, very clean and angular—got up on the side of the bath and looked in the mirror. 'Still looking good,' he said and winked at his reflection before running to the next room.

A sign on the door read 'George's Room—stay out. I mean it.' Archie threw the door open without knocking. A boy of about fourteen with unkempt dark brown, almost black hair sat glued to his TV. Via some miracle that Archie did not quite understand, he appeared to be manoeuvring a heavily armed soldier on the screen with some sort of controller.

George wore headphones with an attached microphone. He stopped talking as Archie entered, turned to the door, and with barely a glimpse of Archie, he froze.

'You must be George,' Archie said to the boy statue. 'Nice to meet you.' He jumped onto George's bed, lay down and had a good stretch. After a few seconds, he got up, rotated George's chair ninety degrees, and then charged out to explore upstairs.

After a quick run around the upper rooms, enough to get his bearings, he ran downstairs and into the large kitchen. It was upmarket—designer cabinets, an impressively large oven, a long central island with a stone top and a couple of cabinets at one end. There were also two comfortable stools on either side.

'Very nice,' Archie said. He ran back to the front room. Edith and Chloe would wake from their trance any second, so he needed to get back into position. Otherwise, if they saw him moving, they'd freeze again, and Archie knew that such things tended to upset humans who disliked unexpected gaps in time.

As he looked at them, reality hit. He might be free, but he was still alone. His features dropped. What was the point of being alive if no one could see you? All he wanted was company and a home. Was that too much to ask?

He sighed and studied Chloe. 'You seem nice, but if you try to keep me locked up, we'll fall out, understand?'

Chloe didn't move.

'Stay completely still if you understand.'

Chloe remained completely still.

'Cool,' Archie said, went to take a step and paused. 'I must be off my furry rocker.' He climbed back onto Chloe's lap.

Archie settled. He had no control over people freezing whilst he was moving, but he could kind of turn himself off. At least, that's how he thought of it. And if he wanted, he could still hear conversation. Once again, Archie appeared to be nothing more than an expensive puppet.

Chloe and Edith blinked. Chloe looked at the bear, aware something had happened but unsure what. Maybe she'd imagined it.

Edith turned to Chloe. 'Sorry, I think my mind went elsewhere for a second. Are you okay?

'Err...' Chloe said, and then added a 'yes,' but she didn't sound entirely sure. She shrugged the feeling off and cuddled Archie. 'He's fantastic.'

There was a noise from George's bedroom, and Chloe looked up at the ceiling. 'What's going on?' George squealed. 'How'd I get over here!'

Chloe grinned. 'I think he's losing.' She wrapped Archie in her arms and lay back, but she couldn't forget that he didn't belong to her... not really. She gently placed him to one side.

Edith could see the doubt on her daughter's face. 'I don't know why my grandfather was so attached to Archie. Maybe I should have returned him, but it seemed to go against his wishes. And I hadn't given him much thought until I saw that documentary advertised.'

Chloe looked up. 'If he left you a famous painting, a famous *stolen* painting, say a Van Gogh, would you return it?'

'Of course.'

'Isn't it the same?'

'So, you think we should return him?'

'We have to, Mum. If we keep him, it's just as bad as if we'd stolen him ourselves.'

Edith considered her intelligent daughter's opinion. 'Maybe I didn't think this through... but okay.'

Chloe nodded sadly. He really was a fantastic bear.

'Do you think we could wait a couple of weeks? Edith asked. 'I'm not sure I can handle a load of awkward questions right now.'

Chloe thought about harbouring a famous stolen bear for a couple of weeks. But then, he'd been in a box for decades. A couple more weeks wouldn't hurt, would it?

'And maybe don't mention that he's famous to George.'

Chloe looked at Archie. He was wonderful. And nothing else this exciting would probably ever happen again in her dull life. 'Deal,' she said and smiled. She looked at Archie. 'He is quite amazing.' She moved Archie's limbs, thinking about the TV show. 'I wonder what he's worth?'

Edith pulled a face. 'I don't want to know.'

'Well, I do. Can we watch the rest of the documentary? It'll be on catch-up.'

Edith picked up her mobile. 'I'll Google it.' She tapped away at her phone and looked at the results. 'Three to five hundred pounds for a reproduction on eBay. There's one locally for four hundred and fifty.'

'Not the same, Mum.' Although even that seemed an awful lot of money, and the real Archie would be worth a lot more. Her mum looked stressed, which Chloe was keen to avoid if her life was ever going to return to any sort of normality. 'It doesn't matter.'

'Good', Edith said.

Chloe toyed with a small snagged thread on Archie's paw.

Edith noticed. 'I better fix that.' She got her sewing kit from the coffee table drawer and held her hand out for Archie. 'It will only take a minute. It would be a shame if he fell apart.'

Chloe reluctantly passed him across.

Edith threaded a small piece of cotton and, via some mystical ability, used it to pull the small snag through to the reverse of the material. It only took a couple of minutes. She gave Archie back.

Chloe sat with Archie until her eyes became heavy, and Edith got up to retrieve the bear.

'Mum,' Chloe whined.

'It's late.'

Chloe held Archie tighter.

'And you've got your school trip tomorrow.'

'Oh yeah.' The trip to the Tower of London had slipped her mind.

'Go on, bed. You look tired.'

Chloe huffed but saw no point in arguing. With only a slight stomp, she walked off and climbed the stairs.

'Stupid tower better be worth it,' she mumbled.

CHAPTER 3

MONDAY MORNING ARRIVED, AND Edith sat at the kitchen island, nursing a cup of coffee.

Chloe entered the kitchen and gave her mum a concerned look. 'Have you eaten, Mum? Coffee isn't food.'

Edith jerked her head back. 'I thought I was the parent!'

'Just checking.'

'I have. Thank you for your concern. And dress warm.'

'Okay.'

Once George joined them, they headed out the door and climbed into Edith's old automatic Ford. Chloe was embarrassed. It was probably the oldest car in London and definitely the oldest on the street. However, twenty minutes later, the car was still reliably chugging along. They had to pass the Tower of London on the way to school, and they both glanced over as they drove past.

'It's a shame I can't just drop you off here,' Edith said.

'There's a bus waiting to take us all.'

The traffic moved, and Edith eased the car forward. 'I know. I do read some of the communications from your school.'

Chloe looked at the tired dashboard, which to her shame, included an actual tape deck. Thankfully, Mum wasn't playing any of her old music. 'You don't need to take me right to the gate.'

'Is the car really that bad?'

'Yep,' Chloe said, nodding like one of those springy toys you some-times find on dashboards.

'Well, don't worry. I can't afford to keep it on the road much longer.' Traffic caused her to stop again, and she turned to admire the ancient structure. 'So, are you looking forward to seeing inside?' she asked, her voice trailing off as the fortress drew her attention.

'Do you think they'll be chopping anyone's head off today?' Chloe asked to see if her mum was still listening.

'What?'

'Just wondered.' Chloe smiled sweetly.

'Not on a Monday,' Edith replied.

After a brief trip in the school minibus, Chloe joined the mass of visitors waiting to enter the Tower. The queue was long. It was cold, and her feet were already hurting.

Annabelle, one of the taller girls on the trip, tapped Chloe on the shoulder.

'We should sit down,' she suggested.

Chloe was reluctant. No one else was sitting down, and she didn't want to get in trouble. However, it would be nice to have one friend. Mum promised they'd visit her old friends once they'd settled—however long that took—but in the meantime, she assured her she'd make new friends. Chloe wasn't sure she wanted new friends; she quite liked her old ones.

Annabelle took her backpack off and used it as a cushion. She looked up at Chloe. 'Come on, then.'

'Okay,' Chloe said, took her backpack off and sat on it. It was weird being surrounded by legs. They pulled their coats tight.

'Chloe, Annabelle, get up, please,' their history teacher, Mr Snark, demanded. He was a slim man with a huge nose and a billowing coat. He reminded Chloe of a vulture.

Chloe shot up.

'Sir,' Annabelle moaned.

'What, Annabelle?' Mr Snark replied. 'It's only been ten minutes. Are your old bones tired already?'

'Yes, sir,' Annabelle replied and dragged herself up.

'How are we supposed to move forward if you're sitting on the floor?' he asked.

Annabelle shrugged.

'What about you, Chloe? Any ideas?'

'No, Sir,' although she assumed it was entirely possible to stand up, move forward a bit and sit down again.

Annabelle shuffled off to find a more entertaining companion. Chloe sighed. She wished she could tell her new classmates about Archie, although if she left out the part about him being famous and missing, it wouldn't have the same impact. And who knew what Londoners found cool? They might have very different ideas to her.

'Sara, is that a mobile phone?' Mr Snark barked at another girl. 'No mobile phones, please. Despite our glorious surroundings, it's still a school day.'

'Can I just finish my text, sir?'

Mr Snark walked towards her with his hand outstretched.

'Sorry, sir, I'll put it away.'

'Good idea. If I see any phones, I will confiscate them until the end of the day. Everybody clear?'

'Yes, sir,' a chorus of voices answered.

'Sir,' said a boisterous boy. 'How do we take photos?'

Mr Snark was stumped; for once, the boy had made a reasonable point. The days of taking a separate camera out were long gone for most casual snappers.

'Err...'

'My mum wants to see lots of photos,' the boy continued, knowing he was on to a winner.

'You make a fair point,' Mr Snark begrudgingly admitted. 'Okay, photos are allowed, unless signs forbid it, of course. But no texting, calling, social media, music, games or any other use of phones I haven't thought of.'

With that, the children with phones took them out and started taking photos.

'And no photos of me, please.'

'Why, sir?' Kyle asked.

'We're here to see this fine building. Do I look like an ancient relic?'

Kyle thought about this.

'No answer is necessary,' Mr Snark said.

The teacher did his best to control things until—to his relief—they finally entered. They passed through a stone archway between two imposing towers, and then Mr Snark ushered them down a slope that branched off to the left into a large dry moat that surrounded the castle. He told them a Yeoman Guard, or Beefeater as they were also known, would give a talk on the history of the Tower.

There were a few groans, but Chloe didn't mind. She secretly enjoyed learning, although kept this quiet for fear of ridicule. Some children thought being clever was bad, which didn't make a lot of sense to her.

The Yeoman Guard joined the growing crowd. He wore a knee-length dark blue tunic with red trimmings. The letters E and R were written across the chest. He also wore a black hat with a round brim. The guard took position before the growing crowd and beckoned stragglers to hurry. 'Excuse me, old people,' he shouted at an elderly couple shuffling towards him. 'Hurry it up, please. I would like to conclude this talk before night sets in.'

There were titters from the crowd.

He surveyed his audience. 'Don't worry. I'll get to the rest of you.'

They smiled warily, and he continued. 'Right, good morning. A bit about myself first. To get to this position, you must have served twenty-two years in the military, usually the army, although we now allow some lesser arms of the forces to join.' He gave a slight smile.

'I was with the army for thirty years before I was granted the honour of my current position. I am one of thirty-seven Yeoman Guards that live and work here....'

He continued to speak about his career before moving on to the castle. 'The first line of defence against potential invaders is the moat. It was also used to dispose of human waste products.'

'You mean wee and poo, sir?' called out one of the boys. The other children giggled.

The guard remained unfazed. 'Yes, wee and poo. These went straight into the moat. There was no sewage treatment in those days. They would also add the odd plague victim, carcass, polar bear or tourist.' He looked at the crowd menacingly, and the children stopped giggling at once. 'This combination sank to the bottom, becoming a boggy pit of human waste and decomposing bodies. It would not have smelt good on a hot summer's day.'

A few children turned their noses up and keenly waited for further detail.

'I mention the polar bear as from the twelve hundreds until 1835, the Tower was used as a zoo to house completely inconvenient gifts from the Kings and Queens of Europe, including a polar bear. Other inconvenient gifts included lions, tigers, bears, kangaroos, monkeys and an elephant.'

Chloe's eyes widened, and she looked around at her surroundings. *An elephant?*

The mixture of history and well-intentioned insults continued as they convened at numerous points within the Tower's grounds, culminating at Tower Hill, where two of Henry VIII's six wives were beheaded.

The Yeoman Guard continued his speech. 'King Henry VIII must have been fond of his second wife, Anne Boleyn, as to ensure she did not suffer, he abandoned the traditional axe and hired an expert swordsman from France to relieve her of her head. On the morning of May 19th, 1536, Anne was led to the scaffold to stand before a crowd of around a thousand people. She was dignified throughout and gave a short speech where she bravely accepted her fate, forgave her executioner and praised the king as a good and gentle prince.'

Chloe clenched her jaw. *He doesn't sound very gentle to me!*

The guard's voice became deadly serious. 'Anne removed her outer robe, knelt and bared her neck. Her head was removed with one perfect clean cut. In fact, legend has it that it was so expertly done that poor old Anne was unaware of her demise, and when the executioner held up her decapitated head to spectators, it continued to talk.'

This image left some children looking a little horrified.

'Of course, it is a Queen's prerogative to have the last word.'

Tales of the condemned continued until they reached the finale. 'The entrance to Jewel House where the Crown Jewels are housed is under that large clock over there in the Waterloo Barracks. It's the largest building of the fortress. So please remember, big building and big clock, and you should be able to find them. Everyone got that?'

'Yes,' they mumbled in response.

'Oh dear,' the Yeoman Guard said. In a louder voice, he repeated, 'has everyone got that?'

'Yes,' the crowd shouted back.

'Good. I will not waste too much time talking about the Crown Jewels as words cannot do them justice.'

'How much are they worth?' a boy asked.

'Why do you want to know?'

The boy shrugged. The guard pointed a finger at him. 'I'm watching you! The jewels have not been officially valued, but most estimates put them at about four billion. That's four thousand million, or a four followed by nine noughts.'

There were small gasps from the crowd. Satisfied he had their attention, he continued. 'The Jewels include the world's largest colourless cut diamond, the Cullinan I, which at five hundred and thirty carats is worth an estimated four hundred million. That's a four and eight noughts. Although that may have gone up since I last looked.'

'What's a carat?' the same boy asked.

'Well, it's nothing to do with the orange vegetable. For diamonds, it is a unit of weight. If your mum has a diamond ring, it's likely to be considerably less than five hundred and thirty carats.'

'I doubt my dad could afford one carrot,' the boy said. 'And I *am* talking about the vegetable!'

The other children laughed.

The guard crossed his arms. 'I'll make the jokes, thank you!'

Chloe imagined a ring with a carrot set into it.

'And if you think any of the jewels would be a nice souvenir to bring home for your mum, then I should point out they are protected by a twenty-two-strong, armed Tower Guard, who will shoot you dead if the need arises. The jewels are kept in bombproof cases behind two-ton steel doors. And at least a hundred CCTV cameras are watching you at all times. Oh, and there's Brad, a complete travesty if you ask me, but I am not consulted on such things.'

'Who's Brad?' a few people asked.

'Brad is more of a *what* than a *who*. You'll find out soon enough. Okay, you lovely lot, that's all I have time for, and it is cold, so I suggest we all get moving. If you have any pressing questions, please do not hesitate to speak to one of my colleagues.'

The crowd dispersed. After nine hundred years of gory history in forty-five minutes, they were ready to explore the grounds for themselves.

But first, the toilets.

After a couple of hours' exploration (of the grounds, not the toilets), the class finally found themselves at Jewel House. As they entered the dark corridors, an excited silence spread between them.

They walked, barely registering the informative histories of the Kings and Queens who had ruled over the last nine hundred years. Chloe learnt that most of the priceless artefacts were collected after 1660 and included the coronation regalia, the items used when a new King or Queen is crowned. Chloe's eyes shone. She'd seen pictures in books or distant shots on TV, but it was not the sort of thing you saw up close, and in a minute, she'd be inches away from the real thing.

But the children hadn't come to learn about history. They'd come to see what four billion pounds worth of treasure looked like.

As they turned the corner into a room that housed the two-ton vault doors, they stopped dead. 'Whoa!' a young lad exclaimed, his eyes like saucers. To the side of the entrance stood a huge rust-red robot knight adorned in plate armour. Its powerful legs were formed from three sections, currently in a crouched stance reducing the machine's intimidating height. It had metal slabs for feet. Its arms were bundles of steel, and two red eyes glowed behind a dark slit in its 16th-century style helmet.

A boy approached, and the robot's gears engaged. It rose to its full eight feet in height and lifted its right arm, which appeared to have a weapon bolted to it. The children stepped back.

'Halt! Identify yourself!' the robot commanded in a deep, electronic voice. The weapon glowed red, and an electric hum intensified as it charged.

'Take it easy, Brad,' said a Tower employee at the robot's side. The machine looked around, its eyes glowing intensely as though assessing targets.

'Stand down,' the employee said and patted the robot on the arm. The robot's eyes calmed to a cooler shade of red as a couple of children retreated further. 'Morning all, my name is James, and the large robot to my right is called Brad, which is short for Big Red Angry Droid.'

Mr Snark shook his head in quiet amusement.

'I know, it's a terrible acronym,' James said. 'It's temporary. We'll ask the public for their suggestions at some point.'

'Is it safe?' Mr Snark asked.

'As long as the jewel enclosures remain intact and no alarms sound, it's perfectly harmless.'

'And if a case gets broken?'

'Laser cannon. Instant death to anyone not authorised to be in this room.' James winked at Mr Snark. 'Okay, feel free to come closer and have a look.'

Chloe and her classmates cautiously approached. Chloe thought the robot was cool but a little scary. As they milled around, the robot's head followed their movement. The machine was the perfect security guard. It never tired and was deadly—a bit like Mr Preston, their gym teacher.

'I don't like it,' a girl said.

'It's okay,' Mr Snark assured her. 'It won't hurt anyone, will you, Brad?' He stepped towards the machine a little too suddenly.

Brad's giant robot head turned to the teacher, and the machine lurched forward. Its heavy step reverberated through the room.

Chloe jumped back, thrusting a hand to her heart. She wasn't alone. Mr Snark jumped in the air, much to the class's amusement. 'That thing's a menace!'

James whispered into his walkie-talkie, 'Hi, can you do a diagnostic check on Brad... No, no problems. Its movements are maybe a little

erratic. I just don't want it freaking out Mr Pearson on Wednesday...
Great, thanks.' He turned back to the crowd and smiled.

Chloe recalled from a lesson on the Tower of London that Mr Pearson
was the Crown Jeweller.

'Time to move, class,' Mr Snark said and hurried them through the
metre-thick steel vault doors.

Chloe dragged herself away from the robot but was now at the back of
the queue. They emerged in a long room with low lighting designed to
show off the jewels, which all had their own light sources. A line of robust
black metal and glass cabinets gradually came into view. Inside were
jewel-encrusted crowns, golden orbs, sceptres, and maces, all perfectly lit
on a black background.

Chloe gasped, and her breathing became shallow as she approached
the treasure. A moving travellator ran along the floor like a horizontal
escalator. Chloe even forgot about the robot as she took in the new
wonders.

As her classmates and other visitors stepped on the travellator, they fell
silent, transfixed as the moving floor moved them down the corridor.

Chloe looked around. There were thick steel bars over the boarded-up
windows and cameras everywhere. The next room opened out a bit, and
she glimpsed—

CENSORED BY ORDER OF HIS HIGHNESS THE KING
The following passages set within Jewel
House are deemed a security risk.
For the protection of the Crown Jewels, these
passages have been struck from the book. We
would like to assure readers that the detailed
and quite marvellous descriptions that
followed were not critical to your enjoyment.

Chloe emerged from Jewel House into the daylight. She had never seen such a display of wealth in her life and wished that photos had been allowed.

Mr Snark waited for the class to emerge.

'Can we go in again, Sir?' Chloe asked.

'No, we cannot,' he said.

'Don't you want to see the robot, sir?' a boy asked.

Mr Snark glared at the boy, and he immediately stopped talking.

A spirited girl smirked and pretended to walk like a robot.

Mr Snark turned to the prankster. 'We could see if the dungeons are still accepting guests?'

The girl looked down at her feet.

'Come on then,' Mr Snark said. 'I'm sure you're all keen to get back to school and find out what your homework is.'

CHAPTER 4

CHLOE SAT IN THE car and told her mum about her visit to the Tower. As she described things, her arms flailed like an over-excited octopus.

'...and the diamond was so huge, I don't think it would've fitted in my hand. It was amazing. And there was this gold salt pot—or was it silver? Anyway, it wasn't like a normal salt pot. It was *this* big!' Chloe stretched her arms out. 'And there was a tower in the centre, and it was full of precious jewels. And there were these long things they called maces—I don't know what they were for, but they were completely gold—and there were crowns, and there was a giant robot called Brad.'

George looked up from the back seat at the mention of a robot but quickly returned to a book he was reading.

'Sorry?' Edith said, sitting forward slightly and glancing at her daughter. 'A giant robot called Brad? Are you making things up?'

'Of course not.'

'Are you sure?'

'There was a giant robot called Brad,' Chloe repeated, feeling a little insulted by the question.

Edith sat back. 'In the Tower of London?'

'He's new. I don't think Mr Snark liked him much. Google it if you don't believe me.'

'I believe you.' Edith continued driving until the traffic ground to a halt. She glanced at her phone, which was attached to the car's air vent by a little plastic clip, and prodded the voice input button. 'Search giant robot and Crown Jewels.'

Her mobile confirmed her request. 'Searching giant row boat and crown ghouls.'

Edith sighed and tried again, stating her words as carefully as possible.

The search results loaded, and Edith's eyes widened. 'Well, I never.'

'Mum, you shouldn't look at your phone while driving.'

'We're stationary, and I'm not even touching it!'

'It doesn't matter.'

'Sorry, Mum,' Edith said to her daughter and rolled her eyes.

'Haha,' Chloe said.

When they returned home, George headed straight toward his bedroom.

'Are you going on your console?' Edith asked.

'Err.... Yes,' George replied, turning back to his mum.

'Don't you have homework to do?'

'I did it in my lunch break.'

Chloe dropped her stuff. 'Can I get Archie?'

Whilst Edith was distracted, George nipped up the stairs.

Okay,' Edith said, not really listening. She went to the front room, sank into the armchair and picked up her newspaper.

Chloe returned with Archie in her arms and placed him on her lap. 'The Crown Jewels are the most amazing thing I have ever seen,' she said, more to Archie than her mum. 'And the robot was cool.' She turned back to her mum. 'And I know something that no one else knows.'

'What's that?'

'The Crown Jewels are cleaned every January.'

'I'm not sure that's a secret.'

'But I know what day.'

Edith looked up from her paper. 'How do you know that?'

Chloe beamed. 'When the robot was scaring Mr Snark, the assistant talked to someone on his radio and said he doesn't want it upsetting Mr Pearson on Wednesday.'

'Who's Mr Pearson?'

'The Crown Jeweller. Once a year, he gets the jewels out and cleans them.'

'Well, that's very clever of you,' Edith said and returned to her paper.

Chloe nodded in quiet agreement with her mum's assessment of her intelligence. 'Oh, and Mum, can I have some cardboard and stuff to make the Crown Jewels?'

'What?'

'Art homework. We have to make two or three items.'

Edith's foot started bouncing up and down on the floor. 'That'll be fun.'

'I can look,' Chloe offered. It was not entirely selfless. It gave her a chance to select the best stuff.

'Best I do it,' Edith said. 'I know what's junk. Did they give you anything to copy, like a photo or a book or something?'

Chloe shook her head. 'Miss Thomas told us to Google it.'

Edith let out a long breath. 'And you know I don't have a computer, don't you?'

'Can't we use Aunt Carol's?'

'No, Chloe, it's private. Some people keep their entire lives on a computer.'

'How about your phone?'

Edith performed a search on her phone and showed her a picture.

Chloe strained to see the image. 'It's a bit small.'

'I'm sure you'll manage.'

'And the picture's all grainy. How old is this phone?'

'Pretty old.'

'But Mum, they were amazing. This makes them look—rubbish!'

'Would you like me to see if the King will pop them round for you to copy?'

 'Yes, please.'

Edith smiled. 'You're a clever girl. I'm sure you can remember how fantastic they were.'

Chloe looked fed up and turned to Archie. 'If you were alive, you'd help me, wouldn't you?' She hugged the bear.

Archie lay over Chloe's shoulder, thinking about her words. He noticed a plaque hanging on the wall:

'Dreaming won't make your dreams come true.'

Archie instantly realised the truth of the message. No matter how much he wanted Chloe to see him, it wouldn't happen by itself. He'd become conscious a couple of episodes before the end of the TV show. Of course, he'd tried to prove his existence to an isolated few away from the cameras, but without success.

Those that saw him froze, and afterwards, there were whispers that he should be disposed of, which didn't sound good. He quickly learnt that he could never reveal the truth. But then things changed. One person saw him.

That person was Jack Goodman—an animator on the show. From Edith and Chloe's conversation, Archie now knew that Jack was Edith's grandfather. Jack said that maybe Archie's millions of fans had willed him into existence. Archie doubted that. Wishes don't come true. Jack also said that if his fans knew him better, they might have reconsidered as Archie's personality was just like on the show—a little bit annoying.

Jack enjoyed teasing him, but Archie didn't mind. That's what friends do.

To prove he was alive, he would have to do something big, something daring. Something that left a human in no doubt that he was an intelligent being and very much alive.

Archie's thoughts returned to Chloe's interest in the Crown Jewels. As an idea formed, he smiled. It was crazy but brilliant.

No, he couldn't.

Or could he?

He mulled it over. If somehow he *gave* Chloe the Crown Jewels, she'd know without any doubt that he was alive, wouldn't she? Who else would have given them to her?

The thrill of the idea soured. He couldn't steal the Crown Jewels. People may object. Although, if he just took a few items, it might be okay. His muzzle curled into a smile.

He had it.

He would *borrow* the Crown Jewels!

Later that evening, Chloe sat in the front room with Archie beside her. She was studying a book called 'The classical drawing atelier,' which she'd found in Aunt Carol's bookcase. Atelier was a posh word for an artist's workshop or studio.

Edith glanced over. 'Isn't that a little advanced for you?'

'Why?'

'Well, it's aimed at adults.'

'I want to draw like an adult,' Chloe said.

'You're a strange child.'

'Thanks, Mum.'

After reading a few more pages, Chloe set the book aside and shifted Archie onto her lap. She studied the texture of his fur, thinking about the lessons from the book. The thought of going upstairs to retrieve her drawing equipment seemed like a lot of effort and prompted an unexpected yawn.

'Early bed for you, I think,' Edith said.

Chloe lifted her head and looked at the clock. 'It's only just gone nine.'

'You could watch TV in bed for a bit?'

Chloe nodded.

'Go on then, and don't forget to clean your teeth.'

'I'm Twelve mum!'

'I'm sorry, but as your mum, I have to remind you for at least another six years.'

'Haha. Can I take Archie?'

'You know you can't. And put Archie back in his box, please.'

'But Mum, it's horrid; it's got bars over the window!'

'I doubt he'll mind. You can leave it unlocked if it makes you feel better.'

Chloe yawned again. 'Fine.' She put Archie back in his wooden casket with the door ajar.

Edith pushed the crate out of sight behind the sofa.

'He can't see there,' Chloe complained.

'Darling, he's not real. And we shouldn't have him on display, especially after that documentary.'

'He wouldn't be on display in my bedroom!'

'He wouldn't last five minutes, either. I'll put him in the spare room.'

Without further debate, Edith lifted the crate and took him to the messiest room in the house. She cleared space on the floor with her foot and put the casket down.

Chloe followed. 'Can you leave the crate door ajar?'

'What for?'

'I don't like him being locked up.' She knew she sounded crazy, but there was something special about him. She just couldn't quite figure out what it was.

'He won't know. But if it makes you happy.' Edith opened the door a little.

'Thanks. Good night.'

'Night.'

Chloe stomped up the stairs past George's room. 'Night, George.'

George blasted some aliens in response.

CHAPTER 5

EDITH LOOKED UP THE stairs at her often-absent son's bedroom door. She climbed the stairs and knocked. There was no response.

She knocked louder. 'Can I come in?'

'Err, I suppose.'

Edith entered. George sat at his games console, a great mop of thick dark brown hair hanging from his head. He wore a snug grey jacket as usual.

'New game?' she asked.

George twisted towards his mother and took a moment to answer. 'Not really.' He waited to hear the reason for the unexpected intrusion.

'Looks cool.'

'I've just died. Want a try?'

Edith moved closer. 'Why not? What are the controls?'

George passed his mum the spare controller and talked her through it. She got it immediately.

'Right, so I have to shoot you before you shoot me?'

'That's pretty much it.'

Edith typed in her initials, *EM*, and selected play. The game's title flashed up on the screen: 'Kill 'em All.'

The screen was split horizontally in two. She had the top half of the screen, and George had the bottom. Edith spent some time familiarizing herself with the bleak city landscape and the weapons and then thought about a suitable strategy. A red dot on the map showed George's approximate location. He was following her.

Edith allowed George to catch up a little, ran around the side of a building, and ducked into an alcove.

The dot came closer.

Seconds later, George ran round the corner after her.

Edith stepped out and shot her son's avatar, who slumped dead to the floor. Red text spread across the screen: *EM killed you.*

George made a harrumphing noise and looked at his mum. 'Why are you so good at these things?'

'Natural talent,' Edith replied.

'Some mums would let their child win.'

'Is that what you want?'

'Yes.'

'Such a little joker.'

He looked her straight in the eyes. 'I'm not joking, Mum.'

Edith smiled. 'So, are you okay? Do you mind being in Aunt Carole's house?'

'It's okay, Mum. I know why we're here. And London is cool.'

George turned back to the console. Evidence of his humiliating defeat was still on the screen. 'So, did you just come up to kill me?'

'I just wanted to check in.'

'Okay,' George said. He studied his mum for a second. 'Are you okay?'

The question surprised Edith. 'I need to find a job, but yes. I think this is what I needed—what we all needed. No more drama!'

CHAPTER 6

ARCHIE WAITED FOR EDITH to settle. He'd long ago learnt that humans enjoy nothing better than relaxing in front of the TV as skilled actors such as himself entertained them, so he didn't have to wait long. Admittedly, he did not do much acting, given that he was not even conscious until the show had almost finished its run, but that was a technicality.

He emerged from his crate and examined his surroundings. A glass chandelier hung from the high ceiling, hinting that the space was probably a dining room in another life. The wall alongside the corridor held a wide, solid bookcase that stretched from floor to ceiling. Piled-up boxes of junk and paperwork occupied the remaining wall space. There was an office desk, reasonably clutter-free, apart from a few books, a carriage clock and a lamp. The room seemed to attract junk, but that was good—it held possibilities. He turned to a window which looked out on the drive. At least he had some natural light.

Archie noticed a creepy object on a cabinet and wandered over for a closer inspection. It was a human skull. He turned it over. An impression at the base read *Made in Malaysia*. It was the closest thing to company he had, so he placed it on the desk and tried to think of a cool name. 'I'll call you Skully.'

Archie went to the desk. It was time to make a plan. He pulled open the drawer and picked a pen from the small selection. There was a stack of paper on the floor, so he removed a sheet and wrote:

1 Find out what day it is.

Archie considered his surroundings. This wasn't a spare room. It was a campaign room—the sort of room where generals planned the defence of the country. Great things would happen here, he knew it. He puffed out his chest and prepared to write something brilliant.

2 Find the Tower of London.

Archie looked at his words, put the plan down, and approached the bookcase. The bottom shelf held all the big books: art, encyclopaedias, dictionaries and books on history. Up from that were books on business, finance, computers—all the boring stuff. And then, there were novels and a travel section at the top.

He found a small nest of wheeled tables: a baby one, a middle one, and a large one, which he arranged in order by the bookcase. For a moment, he wondered whether a stairway of wheeled tables was a good idea. He turned to the model skull. 'What do you reckon, Skully, safe?'

Skully remained silent.

'Be like that,' Archie said, climbed onto the smallest table, stepped to the second, and finally, a short step to the largest, where he stopped to smile at his Malaysian friend.

The top shelf was still too high, and preferring to avoid risky gymnastics, he grabbed a few chunky books, placed them on the table, and stepped on top. At the far right, he spotted a book called *The Tourists' guide to London*. Perfect. Archie reached for the book but couldn't quite make it. Time in the casket had probably left his joints stiff. After a few stretches, he tried again. He just needed one more inch. His paw found the book, and he glanced down to ensure his footing was secure. As he did, the top book slipped to the left, and he to the right. He crashed to the floor with a loud bang.

Archie lay in stunned silence with *The Tourist's guide to London* in his right paw.

He heard the dining room door open and footsteps approach.

Archie scrambled up, shoved the tables away from the bookcase and dropped the book. He then grabbed the plan, climbed into his crate, and shut the door.

'Who's in there?' Edith asked. The door opened in slow motion, and she appeared in the doorway. Her gaze settled on the tables and remained there for half a minute before she dared to step inside. Holding her breath, she curled one finger around the door and pulled it towards her. As it swung from the wall, she peeked around it. There was no one there. Edith breathed again.

She approached Archie's crate. The door was shut rather than ajar. She stared at him.

The moment lasted too long, and Arche wondered whether he should 'come alive' and risk speaking to Edith. Maybe she was the one who would see him. But then he remembered what Jack had once said: *A human, especially an adult human, will never accept a talking toy.*

He wasn't a toy, but ignoring that, what if Jack was wrong?

Edith turned away. She gave the skull on the table a puzzled look but shrugged it off. After checking the window was securely shut, she tidied the tables, flicked off the light, and was about to leave when she spotted *The Tourists Guide to London* on the floor. After thumbing through a few pages, she took the book with her and headed back toward the kitchen.

Archie relaxed. He was glad he hadn't spoken to Edith. She'd freeze, and who knew how many strange events she could take before she decided to lock him away.

It was too dark to risk climbing the bookcase again, so that could wait. He left his crate and unravelled the plan. With the little light coming through the window from a nearby lamppost, he could see enough to write another line

3 Find out where I am.

All he needed was an envelope with their address on it. Impatient to get on with things, he peered out of the doorway and found Edith at the kitchen island, engrossed in *The Tourists' Guide to London*. Archie decided to go for it. He crept out and tiptoed up the corridor to the porch.

There was a flyer for a local pizza parlour on the mat, but nothing with their address. He crept back down the hall towards Edith.

Edith turned his way, and Archie sidestepped into the front room. He took a moment to calm himself and then looked around. The mantelpiece held photos of a woman posing in exotic locations, looking tanned and happy. Edith's sister, Archie, presumed. There was a cool aerial photograph of the house and another of Edith posing with Chloe and George in someone's back garden. Probably their old house.

Archie walked up to the large TV and marvelled at its slim profile. Things had certainly changed over the decades since his show. He made a mental note to look through some of the more educational books in the bookcase and familiarise himself with the modern world.

Someone was coming. Archie tiptoed back to the door.

It was Edith, and she was talking to herself. 'Everything's fine. You're just not used to the house, that's all.'

Archie pressed against the wall as Edith walked through, holding a glass of wine. She stopped about a foot away from him.

'Carole would have mentioned if the house was haunted,' she mumbled.

Archie stood completely still. He was near enough to touch Edith's back. Why didn't he wait until the house was quiet? *Any second now, she's going to turn. She'll freeze, and it won't be long before she wants to 'dispose of me.'*

Edith continued to the armchair, put her glass on the coffee table, and sat. Archie let out a slow breath as Edith aimed the remote and brought up a digital TV guide. He smiled. It was nine forty-five, Monday, the eleventh of January. In two days, Mr Pearson would remove the Crown Jewels for their annual clean.

Archie waited a few minutes and then took a cautious step from his hiding place.

Edith unexpectedly stood, and Archie darted for the door. Had she seen him? Had he left the door swaying? He slipped into the spare room and waited for a second. Edith walked past and onto the kitchen.

All this hiding was stressful, but if Jack was right about not trusting adult humans, he had to be careful. He composed himself, wound the carriage clock, adjusted the arms to show the correct time, and slipped into his crate.

Edith headed to bed just after half past ten, and Archie slipped out. The corridor was eerily dark and quiet. He crossed to the front room, wary of unfamiliar shadows, and eagerly flicked on the light.

The Tourists' Guide to London was now on the armchair.

After a few minutes of flicking through the pages, he decided there was nothing to aid in his quest to 'borrow' the Crown Jewels and left the book where he'd found it. He turned the light off and tiptoed to the kitchen.

Archie paused at the light switch. Edith's bedroom was at the rear of the house—would she notice the light spilling out? He decided to risk it. With a stretch, he flicked the switch and headed into the kitchen. An envelope was lying on a work surface, so he picked it up and memorised the address. He looked around the room, but there appeared to be nothing else he needed, so he quickly switched the light off again.

Back in his room, he turned on the desk lamp. It wasn't too bright, which was good. He looked at the bookcase again and shrugged—he wasn't very good at waiting to do things. He arranged the tables next to the bookcase and placed a small pile of heavy books on top. After a slow and thankfully accident-free search of the bookcase, he found a street map.

Archie unfolded the map on the floor. The maze of streets left him feeling light-headed, but he knew that Chloe and George attended school near the Tower of London, so that was a good place to start. After a twenty-minute search, their address popped out, and he stabbed a furry paw at it. He drew a red line between it and the Tower of London, keeping the route to patches of green where possible. There was one problem—the River Thames. Tower Bridge spanned the river, but Archie suspected it might be popular. He would have to cross the river some other way, although his metal skeleton and swimming were entirely incompatible. The thought made Archie shudder.

He took out his plan and added some more lines.

1. Find out what day it is - Monday.

2. Find the Tower of London - over Tower Bridge (north of here).

3. Find out where I am - 12 Socrates Road.

4. Explore the local area.

5. Organise supplies - a map, a holdall for the jewels, packaging, tools, etc.

6. Wednesday - Borrow the Crown Jewels.

7. Give the jewels to Chloe.

Step six was a little vague, but he knew no other way to gain the information he needed without the right book. He showed Skully the plan. 'Good?'

Skully had little to say on the subject.

Bored with books, Archie explored the boxes of junk. In one large cardboard box, beneath a power drill, a couple of hammers, a box of assorted screws, and a mummified bread roll, he found a long length of curled-up rope. Archie pumped the air with his fist.

Content with the find, he tidied the room, switched off the lamp, and retreated to the crate. He had a lot to think about and was wary of pushing his luck by further exploration.

After a few minutes, Archie changed his mind. He'd spent enough time imprisoned.

It was time to see London.

CHAPTER 7

ARCHIE PULLED BACK THE window latch and eased up the frame. A wall of cold air hit him. He grimaced, braced himself, then put the street map on the ledge and wriggled through the opening. As he touched the icy driveway, he gritted his teeth and wondered if he'd gone slightly mad. He was leaving a warm house to explore an unknown city in the dark. Were these the actions of a sane being? But a small voice in his head told him that if he wanted to prove he was alive, he'd have to be brave. And he should stop acting like a toy bear.

He eased the window shut and flapped his arms to warm up. At least he had a fur coat—it could have been worse. He walked to the end of the drive. The road ahead seemed safe enough, so he set off in the direction of the Tower of London.

After an uneventful few minutes, he found himself in a built-up area—more high-rises, more offices and more danger. A car turned in, its headlights pierced the night, and Archie ran for a tree. It was like being hunted. Only the cars with their bright eyes and snarling grills were the predators.

Archie watched the vehicle disappear and felt a pang of envy—it was probably warm inside the car. A long time ago, he'd pestered his friend Jack to teach him how to drive, but Jack thought it was a bad idea as someone might see him. Archie suspected Jack saw him as a toy bear, not an intelligent being, capable of as much or little as anyone else. Why should the fact that he was small and furry mean he was incapable of driving? Jack had called him 'an infuriating little bear'.

Nevertheless, he took him to a remote patch of waste ground, attached blocks to Archie's hind paws so that he could reach the pedals, and taught him the basics. It had been a fun day. At least he'd enjoyed it—Jack had thought he was going to die.

Further along the street, a young couple strolled hand in hand. Archie watched them enviously. It must be nice to have someone. He jumped over a low wall that ran alongside a block of flats. At the far end, some-thing drew his gaze, and he looked up at a building opposite. A teenage girl wearing a tiger onesie stood at a third-floor window, looking down at him. Archie wondered why she was dressed like a tiger. It occurred to him she might be wondering something similar about him—if she wasn't frozen.

Carrying on, he passed a mini-market, which took up the ground floor of an office block. It was closed and devoid of life. Archie peered through the window at aisles piled high with edible goods. He wondered what it was like to eat food, but it didn't seem necessary. At least not for him.

Rubbing his arms for warmth, he continued walking. He occasionally glimpsed people through their windows, relaxing in front of the TV or eating or playing one of the new video games that obsessed Chloe's brother so much. It looked nice.

As he neared a set of traffic lights, they turned red, and car headlamps soon approached as if answering some unheard call. Archie ducked be-hind a parked car and waited. Part of him wanted to reveal himself. Just jump up and say hi. Of course, they would freeze—there was nothing he could do to prevent that. And if too many people saw him, however briefly, they might feel inclined to investigate. And that could only end badly. He had to be quite selective about who he trusted with the truth. And he hated it.

Archie passed a hotel as a well-dressed couple emerged under a cream awning. They were in their mid-thirties and looked wealthy. They saw Archie and froze, framed in the light from the hotel's entrance. They probably wouldn't remember anything, and if they did, they'd likely keep it quiet. For some reason, adult humans were reluctant to mention seeing a toy bear strolling the streets, even a ruggedly handsome one. The woman had a stylish floral handbag over her arm. Archie eyed it mischievously and slid it off her arm and onto her companion's.

He continued down the road and, a couple of minutes later, heard the man yelp in surprise. Archie turned to see him throw the bag to the ground as if it were a fierce animal hanging off his arm. The woman picked it up and snapped something at him. Archie was too far away to make out the words, but it didn't sound like she was complimenting him. Archie sniggered. *It was only a joke!* He felt slightly guilty, but these little interactions with humans helped him feel real. He couldn't help himself occasionally.

Archie reached a railway bridge supported by a series of arches. He chose the smaller one to pass under and looked at it suspiciously. Cut into the brick tunnel were alcoves with wooden doors painted blue. *Why are there doors under a dingy bridge?* A car approached, and Archie ducked behind a parked vehicle. He waited for it to pass and then took a few steps into the tunnel. It smelt strange—damp brick, mould and something pungent that he couldn't identify and didn't want to. Archie ran and tried his best not to look at the dark little doors just in case there were monsters behind them. But of course, he looked. The monsters remained hidden.

After negotiating a couple more roads, Archie spotted a light in the distance—an old-looking tower. But then he realised it was a bridge—Tower Bridge. He was close, but he'd gone too far. There were too many tourists this way, even in January.

Archie backtracked to a park and followed the path. He ran into a teenage boy smoking a cigarette on a bench. The boy froze, and Archie stubbed out the cigarette and placed a dirty stick between the youth's fingers. 'That's better,' he said.

He continued, and his imagination soon got the better of him. Trees formed dark silhouettes—spindly limbed giants or misshapen beasts with mouths full of teeth. Archie tried to laugh at himself, but it sounded more like a squeak.

A rustle in a nearby dark mass made him jump. He waited for it to reveal whatever horror hid inside. The night felt heavy, like a blanket knitted from shadows. But nothing happened—it was probably just a squirrel or a rat, possibly a fox. He pushed on towards the exit.

Archie sighed with relief. The last patch of green was across the road from him, just a few more minutes of walking. He waited until there were no visible pedestrians or cars and ran across the road, passing under a metal girder that bore the name *Potters Fields*. He reminded himself to be cautious. Isolated incidents wouldn't be disastrous, but he was keen to avoid them.

The park had pleasant pathways with skeletal trees and sparse patches of bush and opened out at the far end. He could see a large glass-domed building in the distance. Its unusual sloped design fascinated Archie. Was the furniture sloped as well? He tipped his head slightly as he imagined walking around the building's interior.

He soon reached the open area, green lawns partially surrounded by shops, offices and towering constructions. Paths led to The Queens Walk, a pleasant promenade and tourist attraction running alongside the Southbank of the River Thames. Archie followed one of these paths, entirely mesmerised by the oily black stretch of water before him and the stunning surroundings.

To his right was the historic Tower Bridge. Two magnificent square towers, like mini castles, stood two hundred feet high and supported a section that opened for river traffic. Two smaller towers on either side of the river connected the rest of the bridge. Lights lit the entire span. It was magical.

Archie approached the river wall, oblivious to anything but the spectacular skyline across the water. And there it was—the magnificent Tower of London, its outer walls bathed in a warm yellow light. Further lamps illuminated a large castle keep, surrounded by four corner towers. Archie smiled.

As he took in the skyline, he felt a presence. He turned to his right and found a well-wrapped man staring at him. He was frozen, his mouth locked open and his eyes wide with shock. Close by, a middle-aged couple holding hands were similarly statue-like. And behind them, a smartly dressed businessman had frozen mid-conversation on his mobile.

Archie turned and saw more people sitting on a long concrete step which ran alongside the walkway. A young man in a chunky jumper and beanie hat had a confused frown. A girl with a bright yellow scarf with her phone aimed at the tower had frozen mid-picture. An older man wearing a high-visibility jacket sat with a cane resting between his legs. He had a bemused smile on his face. There were at least ten people, and they were all statues.

Archie's insides churned. What had he done? He looked around at the human statues. 'Stupid bear,' he moaned and ran back towards the park and the protection of shadows whilst people awoke.

A couple of minutes later, the confused crowd on The Queen's Walk eased back to life. They gave each other vacant looks. Some got up from the steps and staggered forward as if they'd just woken from an unexpected dream.

'Excuse me,' one woman said as she approached another, did err... did something just happen?'

The stranger's eyebrows raised. 'You felt it too?'

One brave man spoke aloud. 'You know, I could swear I saw a large toy bear—'

'You too?' a suited man in a black overcoat remarked with surprise.

'I'm not sure what I saw,' another voice admitted.

A middle-aged woman joined the crowd. 'I saw the bear.'

Everyone agreed that something had happened, although not all recalled seeing a bear. The young man in the beanie hat felt it was too strange to dismiss. He coughed to get everyone's attention. 'We should contact the press.'

'Why?' someone asked.

'They'll think we're complete loons,' another voice commented.

'Because other people may have experienced something similar. Maybe someone has some answers. And besides, perhaps the story will be of interest... there could be some money in it!'

A few nodded their agreement and gave their names and numbers should the press need to contact them. He persuaded an older man to give his contact details, although he was a bit confused and thought he saw an alien, so his testimony was not ideal.

'Anyone else?' the guy with the beanie hat asked. 'The more of us, the better...'

The small crowd quickly vanished, and he took that as a 'no'. He took some pictures of the area and then nervously hurried off as well.

CHAPTER 8

EDITH ARRIVED HOME AFTER the morning school run and threw her keys in a saucer in the hallway. Her face was red, which was normal after navigating London's traffic. She made a cup of tea and then collapsed in an armchair in front of the TV. The local news was playing.

She was about to switch channels when the presenter looked intrigued. 'And we now have a breaking story for you. A crowd—mainly tourists—on the south bank of the Thames suffered an unexplained loss of time last night. Over to you, Judith.'

The feed shifted to a reporter standing at the spot where the phenomenon had occurred. She held a microphone to a man beside her, who was wearing a beanie hat. 'So, tell us what happened?'

The man looked a little embarrassed, but the reporter waited patiently. 'There's not a lot to say. I was out taking a late stroll by the river and stopped to admire the skyline. There was something to my right. I turned and—well, I don't know—froze, I guess. And by froze, I mean like a statue. When I came to and looked around, other people looked as confused as me. The weird bit is the last thing I remember seeing was a toy bear. It was big, maybe four feet tall.'

'A teddy bear?'

'Well, no, it was more realistic, like an expensive puppet from a film. But I saw it so briefly it didn't fully register, you know what I mean?'

The reporter shook her head. 'Not really. And you say others had similar experiences?'

The man moved around to warm up and organize his thoughts. 'Absolutely. There was a crowd of us. Some saw a bear, but some didn't see anything. They just lost time.'

'How odd,' the reporter said. 'What do you think happened?'

He shrugged and pulled his coat tight. 'No idea. I probably would have forgotten about it if it had just been me, but it wasn't, and we couldn't have all imagined it.'

The reporter thanked the man and swivelled to the camera. 'Strange events indeed. We do have collaboration from a couple of other witnesses, but they weren't too keen to talk on air. But if you were here, we'd love to hear from you.'

Edith continued staring at the TV, gave a slight shudder, and then got up and went to the spare room. She tentatively pushed the door open and stepped inside. The room appeared normal, and Archie was in his crate. She studied him, but he was just a puppet. Just as he always had been.

'I'm going mad,' she muttered before returning to the comfort of her armchair.

CHAPTER 9

DETECTIVE EDDIE MASTERS WAS also watching the news, his smart shirt tucked neatly into the waistband of his trousers, despite it being his day off. He liked to look well-groomed and saw no reason his appearance should be any different at home.

When the report finished, he walked towards his home office and nearly tripped over a large brown cat. 'Roswell!' Masters cried. The cat looked at him with an expression that indicated he clearly had the right of way, then gave his shoulder a quick lick and headed off towards the kitchen.

Masters shook his head and continued to his office, where he sat at a leather captain's chair in front of a desk with a green cloth. He turned on a laptop and looked at the wall behind his desk whilst the machine powered up. It was plastered with news clippings:

'UFOs spotted in London.'

'Boys' School Haunted. Three members of staff refuse to return to work.'

'Strange beast sighted on the Moors.'

'Six-year-old child recalls her previous life and tells new house owner about hidden treasure.'

'Top military man admits they recovered live alien.'

And more of a similar nature.

Masters picked up a phone from its charging station on his desk. He dialled and waited.

'Detective Masters,' a grouchy older man said. 'Why are you phoning me? It's your day off, isn't it?'

'Yes, boss. Did you watch the news today? People reported an unexplained loss of time down on the South Bank by Tower Bridge.'

'Yes, I saw it. Utter nonsense.'

Masters played with the computer mouse on his desk as he considered his wording. 'But what if someone could incapacitate people for brief periods? It would be a formidable weapon, sir.'

'I can't believe a man of your age and intelligence has an interest in all this.'

'With respect, sir, this wasn't one man. A whole crowd experienced it.'

'So says one man.'

'I understand a couple of others confirmed the event,' Masters said. 'I think it's worth talking to this man and anyone else we can find who was at the scene. Compare stories. Maybe check any CCTV footage from the area.'

'I tell you what, Masters, if anyone else sees a teddy bear and then freezes like a statue, the case is yours. Okay?'

'Sir, I was hoping—'

'That will be all, Masters. Why don't you try to enjoy your day off? You know your problem, don't you?'

'No, sir.'

'You spend too much time on your own.'

The line went dead. Masters sighed and looked around his empty house. He replaced the phone and again looked at the newspaper clippings on the wall. It was a little soon to add the story, but he would look out for developments with interest.

CHAPTER 10

FOLLOWING AN UNEVENTFUL DAY at school, Chloe was home and pondering the important question of dinner. It felt like a junk food kind of day.

'Pizza!' she said. 'With Chips.'

'Pie and mash,' George requested, appearing as if by magic at the mention of food.

Edith opened the fridge door to check on supplies. 'I think you're both out of luck. I need to go shopping. How about a nice healthy jacket potato with cheesy beans and salad?'

'With chips?' Chloe asked.

'You want potato with a side portion of potato?'

'Yes, please.'

'I don't think so.'

'Can I get Archie, then?' Chloe asked, knowing that sometimes she could minimise debate by asking for two entirely unrelated things in quick succession.

Edith paused before answering. 'If you like.'

Chloe returned moments later with Archie under her arm.

George looked at her. 'What do you see in that tatty old bear? Aren't you a bit old?'

'No! He's special.' She wanted to elaborate but remembered she couldn't.

Edith gave her a warning look. Chloe gave her mum the slightest nod.

'He's not special,' George said. 'He's old and smelly, and he's falling apart.'

Chloe glared at George. 'No, he's not!'

'Look at his feet, or paws, whatever you call them.'

Chloe looked at Archie's hind paws. They were looking the worse for wear.

'How did that happen?' Edith asked. 'Have you been playing with him?'

'No!'

Edith's eyes narrowed. 'Are you sure?'

'Yes! I've been at school.'

Edith scrutinized Chloe. 'What about last night?'

'I was tired. I fell asleep.'

'Someone has,' Edith said. 'What about you, George?'

'What about me?'

'Have you been playing with Archie?'

George's mouth fell open. 'Why would I play with that skanky old bear?' He exhaled in disgust and left.

Chloe smelled Archie's fur. 'He doesn't smell; he just needs a little airing.'

Edith looked at Archie's paws again. 'Someone's been playing with him. Unless he just got up and went for a wander around London by himself?'

Chloe shrugged. 'Well, it wasn't me.'

Edith breathed in and out slowly. 'Did you hear the news today?' she asked.

'The news is depressing.'

'Just no would be fine. Some people in London said they felt like they'd lost time, like they'd been frozen.' She hesitated. 'Have you ever experienced anything like that?'

Chloe remembered meeting Archie, and it did feel very much like she'd lost time. But that was impossible, wasn't it? You lose socks or keys. You don't lose time. 'What do you mean frozen?'

Edith went silent. 'Doesn't matter. Probably just a silly story.'

Chloe was happy to avoid this conversation. The less stressed her mum was, the better. 'I'm going to start my homework with Archie.'

'Okay.'

Chloe waited.

'Yes?'

'You said you would get me some cardboard and stuff.'

'Oh, *that* homework.' Edith massaged her temples. She rushed off and rummaged through cupboards and bins, dragging out anything that could be useful.

After a ten-minute search, Edith amassed a collection of cartons, cereal boxes, toilet roll inserts, a couple of old dresses, some shiny gold Christmas paper on a long tube, a washing-up liquid bottle, some string, and even some old dress jewellery that had little value. 'Will this do?'

'No diamonds?' Chloe asked.

'Sadly not.'

'Then it will do.'

'Thank you, Mum,' Edith reminded her.

'Thanks, Mum.'

'You're welcome.' Edith also handed across her mobile phone.

Chloe looked at it.

'I saved a few pictures of the Crown Jewels.'

Chloe considered the small device with obvious distaste. 'Thanks.'

She took Archie into the front room, plonked down on the couch, positioned Archie beside her, and scrolled through the pictures her mum had saved. She felt rather uninspired by the tiny images. She showed one to Archie. 'What do you think?'

Archie remained still.

'Yeah, I know. Rubbish.' She pulled the coffee table closer and got to work. The cardboard roll from the wrap was a little wide for the sceptre, so she cut along its length, tightened it up, then taped it and covered it with gold paper. It looked good, although the little silver stars dotted over it were not very authentic.

With intense concentration, she cut two heart shapes out of cardboard, cut out the middle, and added some slits so that the two pieces interlocked in a clasp. She found the fake precious stone from her mum's dress jewellery and glued it within. Finally, she topped it off with a cardboard cross covered in gold and silver paper and glued the clasp and cross to the rod.

Not bad, but if she'd had better reference material, it could have been amazing. She put the sceptre to one side, cut out a piece of card for a crown and wrapped it around her head. She'd have to cut the various intricate parts to shape once she'd measured it. Maybe she could also find some purple cloth to line the inside of the crown. After all, she was getting older—cardboard alone would not quite do.

'Dinner!' Edith called.

Chloe looked at the clock. How had over an hour passed already? She picked up a pencil, ready to mark where the cardboard overlapped.

'Chloe! Dinner!'

Chloe sighed and put down the cardboard.

Dinner passed uneventfully. Chloe didn't feel like talking to George, and he had an important video game battle scheduled, so he ate his meal in minutes.

Edith's mind was elsewhere. Chloe was used to that.

After dinner, Chloe returned to the front room with Archie and spent some more time on the jewels, managing to cut the crown to shape and wrap it in gold paper. She then made a point of watching the news.

They showed the same clip from earlier. A man at Potters Fields talked about losing time. He also said he thought he saw a bear puppet before it happened. Mum hadn't mentioned that bit. And it was strange how it coincided with Archie coming into her life. But it was probably just a coincidence.

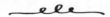

Archie remained still and toy-like whilst he watched the news with Chloe, but he was starting to feel a little impatient. And he was still angry about George's words before dinner. *Skanky Bear. He was a global superstar!*

There was one more thing he could try a little later to attract Chloe's attention. He was a little hesitant before, as George may get the blame. But that didn't matter now—George deserved it.

His mind went back to the news. Although hearing people talking about him was a little unsettling, it did present one advantage. Maybe Chloe would be a little more inclined to believe he was real. She certainly hadn't quite seemed herself after she'd watched the clip.

Archie was thinking about this when Chloe turned to him. With a pained expression, she studied his face and asked, 'Was it you?'

Archie could hardly believe what he was hearing. Did she know? He jumped off the couch and turned to Chloe. 'Of course it was me! How many talking bears do you have in London?'

Chloe was frozen, incapable of interacting with Archie.

'Chloe!' Archie urged. He tapped her on the knee. 'Hello!'

She remained silent.

Archie growled with frustration. 'I'll prove I'm alive, you'll see.' He climbed back onto the sofa beside her and became still. After a couple of minutes, Chloe came round.

She blinked and looked at Archie. 'What are you?' she whispered and picked him up to return him to his crate.

Archie remained still, but inside he was hurting. How long would it be before she was too scared to hang out with him? Or worse, how long until she locked him up?

On Chloe's way to the spare room, Edith stopped her.

'Bored with Archie already?' Edith asked.

'I've just got things to do,' Chloe answered quietly. After a second, she turned back. 'Mum...'

'Yes?'

'Do you think those people standing by the Thames really froze?'

Edith looked at Archie. 'After seeing a toy bear?'

They looked at each other for a moment, and then Chloe pretended to laugh. 'Of course, they didn't. It's stupid.'

'It seems unlikely,' Edith said in agreement, but she looked unsure.

Chloe put Archie away in his crate and headed to her room.

That evening, after everyone retired, Archie let himself out of his casket. His limbs felt sluggish, and his heart heavy with worry. He plodded around the room, thinking about the task ahead. All he had to do was get to the Tower of London without freezing half of the city, break into an impenetrable fortress, get past the armed guards, bypass the massive vault doors, and then return home with the jewels whilst avoiding soldiers, police and anyone else that happened to be looking for him.

It was insane. But how else could he prove he was alive?

He walked to the window overlooking the drive and stared at the night sky. For some reason, he found the stars comforting. But time was running out.

Before he committed to Plan A, there was one thing left to try.

Archie found some paper and wrote a brief note. He folded it in half and wrote Chloe's name on the front.

He then took the note upstairs and placed it on the drawers beside Chloe's bed. Now all he could do was wait.

CHAPTER 11

AFTER A POOR NIGHT'S sleep, Chloe woke feeling grouchy. She opened her eyes a fraction, and a piece of paper on the drawers by her bed came into focus. It had a name on it—her name. Sliding her legs over the side of the bed, she took the note and unfolded it. She scowled, making her eyebrows knit together, and stormed downstairs still in her nightdress.

She burst into the kitchen. 'Mum, look what George left on my chair!'

Edith stopped what she was doing and took the note from Chloe. She unfolded it:

I am alive, but no one can see me. I will prove it if I have to. Archie x.

'I'm sure it was just a joke.'

'It doesn't matter,' Chloe said. 'He's not allowed in my room without permission.'

'George, can you come down for a second, please?' Edith shouted.

'One minute,' he yelled back.

Edith looked at the note again. 'It's not his writing.'

'So? He disguised it. Maybe he's developed his first brain cell.'

George eventually arrived in the kitchen.

'What's this, George?' Edith asked and handed the note over.

George took the note, read it, and with a confused expression, handed it back. 'Nothing to do with me.'

'You didn't write it?'

'Why would I write that? It's ridiculous. How can a toy bear be alive?'

'It must have been you!' Chloe barked.

'I wouldn't do anything so stupid.'

'So, you're saying that Chloe wrote it?' Edith asked.

'Err, yeah!'

Chloe gritted her teeth. 'I didn't!'

Edith exhaled heavily. 'Maybe you should both stay in your rooms after school until you work it out.'

'Fine by me,' George said.

'With no console,' Edith added.

George's jaw dropped. 'And George, you should ask permission before entering Chloe's room.'

'So much for innocent until proven guilty.'

Edith crossed her arms. 'Well, I know I didn't write it. Say sorry to your sister.'

George glared at Chloe and then back to Edith. 'Fine, you've clearly made your mind up. It wasn't me, but sorry.' He spat the word *sorry* out like it was poisonous and then stormed off.

Edith shook her head. She was about to shout after George but decided to leave it. 'Great start to the day.'

'He doesn't sound very sorry,' Chloe said.

'I admit he could have been a bit more sincere, but can we please leave it? I'll have him whipped later.'

Chloe huffed. 'Don't forget.' She threw the note in the bin, but there was something niggling at the back of her head. George was almost too convincing. But, of course, he must have written it. Who else would have done it? 'Can we go to school, please?' she asked her mum.

'As soon as you've had breakfast, although we are a little early. You may also want to change out of your nightdress.'

Chloe ignored the sarcasm and dished out some cereal. She poured cold milk over it and scoffed the lot in record time. 'Done,' she said, and a milk line dribbled from her mouth.

'How attractive,' Edith said and tapped at her mouth to show Chloe she may want to wipe her face.

Edith went to the stairs and shouted towards George's bedroom. 'Be ready in ten minutes, George!'

'Do I have to get in the car with *her*?' he shouted.

Edith sighed. 'Yes, you do!' She returned to the kitchen.

Chloe shook her head with annoyance. 'Listen to how sorry he sounds. Practically weeping.' She left the table and headed for her bedroom, deciding that if her brother was determined to lie to her and Mum, then she was determined to have nothing to do with him.

Archie backed away from the door where he'd been listening to the conversation. Well, that was a disaster. He sank to the floor. He knew George might have been blamed and had hoped it would provide some small satisfaction in return for George's unkind words yesterday. It didn't. Perhaps he should have sat in Chloe's bedroom with the note until she woke. She'd have found him, pen in paw. But would it have made any difference? Probably not. She'd have just thought that George had put him there. And that wouldn't have gone down too well either.

Not for the first time, he wondered why he was alive.

A little while later, Archie peeked out the spare room window as Edith and Chloe pulled out of the drive. His thoughts returned to the Tower of London. After seeing the structure for real, his original plan seemed inadequate, so he returned to the bookcase. There were plenty of books about the Kings and Queens who'd lived at the Tower. Even more about the residents who met their end there, but he needed something he could use.

Once again, he arranged the three tables to form some steps and climbed up. He thumbed through the few travel books he hadn't already looked at and quickly realised it was time to admit defeat. He looked towards the desk. 'Any ideas, Skully?'

Skully had nothing to offer. Archie tried to return the *Filthy Rich Guide to London*, which he'd removed, but the book refused to go back. He held on to an upper shelf, pulled himself up and pushed his paw to the back. There was something there.

There was no one in for him to disturb if he fell, so he stretched and eventually pulled out a few screwed-up pamphlets. He straightened them out. They were all attractions in London, but one caught his eye: *The Tower of London, a visitor's guide.*

Archie punched the air. 'Now we're talking!' He jumped down, quickly returned the books from the top of the table to the bookcase, and then sat on the floor and opened up the pamphlet. It included a map of the Tower of London, with each structure identified. Archie wiggled his bum in a little seated dance.

The jewels were kept in Jewel House, part of the large Waterloo Block. The entrance he needed was underneath a large overhanging clock. Unfortunately, there were no photos of the jewels or their enclosure. There was also no information about the security arrangements. An unfortunate oversight, he thought, but it was a start.

CHAPTER 12

DETECTIVE ED MASTERS HEARD the letterbox bang and walked down the hallway to retrieve his morning newspaper. He returned to the kitchen and poured some coffee beans into a large steel coffee maker. The machine made various whizzes, bangs and slurping noises as he flicked through the pages.

He grabbed his coffee, added half a sugar and ambled towards the dining room. Halfway there, he paused as something caught his attention, then continued to the table and laid the newspaper out.

Following the plea to the public for further information regarding the incident at Potters Fields, a few witnesses had sent in drawings of a toy bear. One stood out—the artist had drawn a bear wearing striped trousers, a shirt and braces. But more importantly, the artist had identified a key feature: a swathe of white fur which ran from the bear's neck to the top of its chest.

Masters recognised the image, but being a disciplined man, he went to his office and fired up his laptop. He googled *The Amazing Archie*. The photos confirmed his suspicion. The last thing sightseers had seen was a bear puppet from an old children's TV show or at least something that looked very similar. He also read that the bear had been missing for decades.

He reread the article and decided it now warranted a place in his collection. He found a pair of scissors, cut the story out and pinned it to his office wall alongside the other mysteries. The clippings held his attention for a bit, but work was waiting, and he hated being late. He gave the story one last glance. *Where are you now, Archie?*

CHAPTER 13

EDITH RETURNED HOME FROM the morning school run with a newspaper under one arm. She settled down with a cup of tea in the front room and, after flicking through the latest political scandals, unexpectedly turned to a drawing of Archie. She choked on her tea and slammed the mug down.

Once the coughing had subsided, she stomped into the spare room and thrust the paper in front of Archie's crate. 'Was this you?'

Archie didn't move.

Edith stared at him a moment longer. Finally, the tension eased out of her body. 'I'm losing it.'

She rotated Archie's crate, so she didn't have to look at him. 'You're going to have to go, Archie.' As she turned to leave, something stopped her. There was a repetitive, unfamiliar ticking. The source was a carriage clock—it even showed the correct time.

Edith stared at it. Finally, with a dismissive shake of her head, she left, slamming the door behind her.

Chapter 14

Archie spent the rest of the day packing his rucksack but treated Edith like an unexploded bomb. He kept his distance. Despite the frightening prospect of what he had to do next, he was relieved when three o'clock came, and he could finally escape the confines of his room.

After one last look at his campaign quarters, he took a deep breath, grabbed a large rucksack and passed it through the open window. He lowered it to the ground and then turned back to the room. 'See ya, Skully,' he said with a sad lilt as if he didn't expect to come back, then clambered through himself and gently slid the window shut behind him.

Edith's car was in the driveway, the boot facing away from the road. He took a wire hair clip from his pocket, straightened it out and leaned on the car boot with his hand over the lock. He wasn't entirely sure this would work, but it worked on TV and Edith's car was quite old. The boot popped open before he'd even inserted the wire.

Archie blinked with surprise. The car was so decrepit it didn't even lock! He threw the hair clip into the boot in disgust. The front door to the house clicked shut, so he chucked the rucksack in and dived in after it. He found a rusty hole and used it to pull the boot shut.

The car sank a little as Edith climbed inside. She turned the ignition, and the engine whined as if objecting to being woken, but it settled down as they pulled away.

The boot gave the occasional rattle, and Archie found that if he gave it a push, he could see through a small gap. He watched the house shrink into the horizon and wondered if he would see it again, but there was no turning back now.

He shifted to try and make himself comfortable, but there was only so much he could do in a metal box above old-fashioned suspension. Music began to pump from the car's speakers—an exciting, jumpy melody, which seemed quite fitting for his adventure.

As the car turned a corner, Archie rolled into his rucksack. 'This was a stupid idea,' he moaned as he untangled himself. He huffed and pulled out a superhero mask he'd found. It had probably belonged to George or Chloe at some point, but right now, he had greater need. And it's surprising how a silly mask can make you feel like a different person—a braver person. The mask was red with two holes for his eyes. Not the best disguise ever, but nevertheless, he pulled it over his head and adjusted the elasticated band until it felt comfortable. Also hidden in his rucksack were packing material, rope, a utility knife, armbands, and a note. All the essentials needed to pull off the heist of the century.

Edith crossed London Bridge, and the car eventually stopped in traffic outside the Tower of London. Archie found the cable connected to the boot latch and gave it a tug. The boot obligingly popped open. 'Cool,' Archie whispered as he climbed out, keeping the boot as low as possible as he slipped onto the road. There was no screech of surprise from Edith's direction, so it appeared he'd escaped unnoticed.

Archie straightened his mask and looked at the car behind Edith's. The driver was frozen, his eyes wide and glassy, cheeks pinched like a goldfish sucking a chilli.

He turned towards the Tower of London. The name was misleading—it was not just a tower. There were towers, turrets, barracks, and other buildings. There were even homes for the guards. And they were all protected by two surrounding walls and a moat.

Archie readied himself and ran across the road, glancing briefly at a young boy looking out the car window and playing a game with his parents. 'I spy with my little eye, something beginning with—' The lad didn't get to finish the sentence.

As Archie skirted around the building, more tourists froze. His hopes of going relatively unnoticed at one of the most visited tourist attractions in the world had perhaps been a little optimistic. But it was too late now.

He found the queue for entry and hid behind a woman's legs at the back, but before he'd even considered his next move, another woman looked at him and froze. Her partner let out a gasp of surprise. As he looked for help, his eyes found Archie, and he froze also. Soon the entire queue was frozen. Archie may as well have danced up to the entrance singing show tunes.

Archie wound his way through the frozen people, past the guards' stations and under Middle Tower—two sturdy round towers joined by a square building with an arched passage. He glanced at a flat sculpture above the arch. Two lions stood on their hind legs on either side of a shield and crown. At least the Tower no longer held real lions to deal with, just seven ravens, according to the travel guides. The same guides also warned that the kingdom and the Tower of London would fall if the six resident ravens ever left the fortress. The seventh raven was a spare.

He followed a bridge with a stone wall on one side and railings on the other across a dry moat to the Byward Tower. It was similar to the first Tower, except it contained a portcullis—a heavy spiked gate to deter invaders. Archie envied the tourists. It would be nice to explore at leisure and maybe lower the portcullis. There was a slight chance he might skewer a few tourists, but he'd be very careful.

Archie emerged from the arch between the pentagon-shaped defensive walls. A young girl holding her mother's hand looked at Archie. Her hand became rigid, and her mother looked down. She squealed. 'Baby, are you okay?' But then she spotted Archie, and she also became a statue.

Archie consulted his map and then made his way to the inner ward—a grassy area with trees dominated by a huge square tower with turrets and domed roofs at each corner. It was known as the White Tower. A wooden staircase ran up the side of the building, and Archie wondered what secrets were inside, but that would have to wait for another day. Frozen people were dotted around—it was time to move.

After getting his bearings, he continued to one of the Tower of London's less talked about features—the men's toilets. Inside, he squeezed past a couple of now-frozen men and locked himself in a cubicle.

And he waited.

After a couple of minutes, he heard the two men return to life, and one nervously spoke to the other. 'I don't suppose you saw a b—'

'Yes?' the other man asked.

'It doesn't matter.'

'No, please go ahead.'

'It's fine. I'm probably imagining things.'

'Yes, that could be it....'

'Why? Did you see something?' the first asked.

'No, nothing, you?'

Outside, people were moving again. There was some nervous conversation but no screams, so he hoped he might be alright. And if the two men outside his cubicle door were typical, maybe he didn't need to worry.

Time dragged inside the cubicle, but eventually, the tourists left, and Archie knew it was time to emerge. He snuck out into the winter night. The grounds felt different without crowds of visitors chatting and snapping photos. He could almost imagine he'd travelled back in time, and the White Tower still held its unlucky prisoners. Although the building was undergoing some repairs, which slightly spoilt the illusion. Archie took advantage of the situation and ran for a stretch of scaffolding covered in white tarpaulin.

He'd almost reached the walls when lights all over the Tower suddenly lit.

Archie stopped. Surely no one had seen him? They would just freeze, wouldn't they? He turned his head slowly, but no one was watching, and he let out a relieved breath. The lights must be on some sort of timer. Or maybe there was a sensor which measured how dark it was. He'd read about something similar in one of the encyclopaedias back home. The world has grown clever in the last sixty years.

He continued to the White Tower, pressed himself against the stone and manoeuvred around until he was opposite Jewel House. He pulled a utility knife from his backpack, made a slice in the tarpaulin and brought one eye up to the slit.

It was another half hour before four armed soldiers escorted Mr Pearson, the Crown Jeweller, to Jewel House. Two soldiers took him inside while the other two stopped, spun around to face him, and readied their rifles.

The sight of the two lethal weapons sent a shiver through his metal skeleton, and for once, he prayed they would freeze when he left his hiding place. He estimated it would take about ten minutes to open the vault doors and remove the Crown Jewels from their bombproof cabinets, so he noted the time on the large clock above Jewel House and waited.

Finally, the time was up, and Archie looked again at the soldiers, took a deep breath, and sprinted towards them.

The soldiers' grips on their rifles shifted.

Archie's eyes widened behind his superhero mask.

But there was no movement. The soldiers were frozen, incapable of moving even a finger. It was just nerves—he'd imagined it.

Archie ran through an arched stone doorway into Jewel House. The building was kept intentionally dark to show off the various displays and cabinets, which all had their own lighting. The walls were solid stone, cold to the touch, and seemed to breathe out history. Archie passed portraits of kings and queens from past centuries. He followed the path until he reached two soldiers on either side of the massive vault doors. The soldiers stood, feet apart, rifles held at waist height. Both stared forward with icy expressions, although one had a slightly raised right eyebrow.

As scary as the soldiers were, they were not as terrifying as the enormous robot that stood with them. Archie's jaw dropped as he took in the creature—an armoured metal knight of alarming proportions with powerful legs and muscles formed from bundles of steel. He would not like to meet this creature when it was awake.

Archie looked up at its head and wondered what was behind the dark slit in its helmet.

He tore himself away from the monster. The jewels had to come first. Archie walked through the vault doors and into the main enclosure. A line of glass cabinets ran down the centre. Archie knew the soldiers would wake in a couple of minutes, so he had to act quickly. Ahead of him was the Crown Jeweller. The Coronation Regalia lay before him on a long table cushioned by lengths of silk. There were assorted bottles, brushes, and cloths down one side and a lit magnifying glass on a stand in the centre of the table.

The Crown Jeweller had been about to sit on a stool but hadn't quite made it. He'd frozen mid-perch upon seeing Archie.

Archie marvelled at the jewels before him. They were beautiful. He shook himself out of his semi-trance and opened his rucksack. The Coronation Regalia would be perfectly acceptable. He chose three items, all of which he recognised from the history books he'd read back in his campaign room.

The first was the Imperial State Crown, an ornate gold, silver and platinum crown adorned with sapphires, rubies and the Cullinan II diamond.

The second he chose was the Sovereign Orb. It resembled a shining golden ball decorated with sapphires, rubies, emeralds, amethyst, diamonds and pearls.

Finally, he picked up the Sovereign Sceptre with Cross and examined it. The gold sceptre was decorated with diamonds, rubies, emeralds and sapphires. A heart-shaped clasp held the huge Cullinan diamond, topped with a diamond-studded cross. Archie paused—he'd read it was the largest colourless cut diamond in the world. He gulped and forced himself to move.

Archie wrapped the precious items in cloth, then put them in doubled-up bin bags, and finally, he wrapped tape around the outside. He laid out a note on the table which read: *Just Borrowed.*

He returned through the steel passage and stopped at the giant robot. Again, he glanced at the slit in its helmet. He had to know what was in that dark cavity. There was motion outside, so he lowered his rucksack and ran out. The confused soldiers turned towards him.

'Give me a couple more minutes, would you?' Archie asked politely.

The soldiers both froze.

Archie returned, re-freezing the soldiers by the vault doors as he passed. He approached the machine, determined to get a closer look. The robot was in a relaxed position, so Archie climbed onto its heavily armoured knee and reached to the top of its chest plate to pull himself up. His paws brushed over a steel badge with the name *B.R.A.D.* stencilled across it. As he moved, some of his hair caught in one of the overlapping plates. Archie freed himself and lost a small patch of fur, which slipped inside a vent into the heart of the machine. He winced.

He remembered Mr Pearson had a stool he wasn't currently using, which would be a far more sensible way of getting a better look.

Archie jumped down and ran back to Mr Pearson, who was still poised, ready to sit.

Meanwhile, the hairs Archie had lost settled onto the robot's inner circuit boards. As they lay there, a strange blue energy escaped from the roots and drifted like smoke through the circuits.

Within the machine, lights flickered on.

Motors powered up.

Steel fibres tightened.

Archie dragged Mr Pearson's stool back through the immense vault doors and set it down next to the robot. He clambered onto the stool for a better view. Even then, he was barely at chest height with the robot.

The machine attained full power and rose to its full height. Its eyes suddenly glowed red as electricity coursed through its circuits. It lowered its enormous head towards Archie.

'Oh, dear,' Archie whimpered. He stepped backwards and fell off the stool, hitting the floor hard. He cried out in pain.

'Intruder found,' the robot bellowed. 'Please state the override code within fifteen seconds to avoid lethal force.'

Archie tried to run for the exit.

The robot swung its arm, sending Archie flying through the vault door and into the main jewel enclosure. He landed on his back and then realised something. 'You can see me!'

'Thirteen seconds remaining.'

'Eleven...'

'No, wait! I need to know how,' Archie pleaded.

'Nine seconds remaining.'

'Just tell me, please!'

'Seven.'

The machine squatted down to manoeuvre itself through the vault doors. 'Five.'

Archie stepped backwards. 'Look, keep the jewels. I'm sensing some hostility—'

'Three.'

The cannon attached to its right arm glowed. The accompanying hum grew in pitch and volume.

'One. Extermination imminent.'

'Stop,' Archie pleaded.

The machine fired a laser beam at Archie, but he moved with a fraction of a second to spare.

Archie backed against a cabinet containing a gold crown.

The robot pointed its cannon at Archie again.

There was no escape. Archie closed his eyes. This was it—today was the day he died.

He waited.

But nothing happened.

Archie opened one eye. 'You can't shoot the cabinets, can you?'

The machine raised its foot and stomped toward him. Each step echoed throughout the room. Archie searched for an escape, but the robot kept coming.

The robot grabbed Archie with a mighty hand. Iron fingers closed on a handful of fur and lifted him to its eye level.

Archie stared into the creature's eyes—two discs of glowing red. 'Please....'

The robot lifted its remaining arm and pointed the cannon at Archie. The weapon began to glow brighter.

Archie kicked out with all his might, leaving a fistful of fur in the robot's iron fist. He fell seven feet, slamming into the floor. Grunting with pain, Archie rolled back onto his feet and sprinted through the vault door, grabbing his rucksack containing the jewels on the way.

As he neared the exit, a searing red beam of light pierced his ear. 'Owwww!' The robot crouched again to manoeuvre its bulk through the vault door. Archie had seconds and ran past the soldiers who had just woken. 'Sorry!' he yelled as the soldiers froze once more.

The robot stopped at the entrance to Jewel House, its massive bulk silhouetted within the stone frame. But it would not, or could not, leave the remaining jewels.

Archie looked around. The exits would be locked, so he ran through the enclosure towards the outer wall and up some stone steps. He charged along the battlement, looking for something to attach a rope to, and found a light in a metal bracket bolted to the wall. The bracket appeared to be strong. Archie had a quick scan around and decided it was his best chance.

There was a commotion below. The soldiers must have discovered the robot in the doorway. Any second, they would find some essential items missing from the Crown Jewels collection.

An alarm sounded, similar to an air raid siren—a horrible sliding pitch that went up and down and chilled the heart.

Archie tied the rope to the bracket using a quick-release knot and gave it a tug to test it was secure.

A booming voice competed with the siren. 'We have an intruder. Jewel House has been breached!'

Loud footsteps and slamming doors reverberated through the night as Yeoman Guards and soldiers stopped what they were doing and ran towards Jewel House. Even without the announcement, everyone knew what the siren meant; the impossible had happened. The Tower came alive with shouts of disbelief and outrage.

Footsteps approached the battlements.

Archie heaved himself over the top, keeping tension on the rope as he leaned back and used it to walk down the wall.

A head appeared over the wall. 'Stop or I'll—'

The voice came to an abrupt stop.

'Freeze?' Archie suggested. He hit the ground and gave the rope a shake. The knot came undone, and the rope fell to his feet. He gathered it up.

Shouts and whistles grew louder, and someone shone a powerful torch over the battlements.

Archie looked out over the river. There had to be another way.

Flashing lights filled the night, and sirens wailed as police cars sped across Tower Bridge. The authorities had acted swiftly.

Archie approached the railings situated on the river wall and peered over. It looked like a long way down. A sign read, *Warning, strong currents may cause death.* Archie gulped, but the noises behind him weren't getting any quieter. With an anguished sigh, he undressed and shoved his clothes into the rucksack. A frosty breeze ruffled his fur as he pulled a pair of armbands out, hurriedly inflated them and slid them on.

Archie shook with fear. The soldiers' continued to scream instructions to each other, and a shaft of torchlight sliced through the winter night beside him, picking out ripples in the Thames. After checking his bag was secure, he clambered onto the railing and eyed the water beneath him. *This was a bad idea!*

He stepped off and dropped into the icy Thames with a splash. Instantly his limbs were immobilised by the freezing water. Something thumped rapidly in his chest, and it took all his will not to panic. He forced his limbs to move.

With each stroke, he felt heavier, colder and more exhausted. The far bank seemed impossibly distant, and the river was intent on taking him away. By the time he'd reached halfway, his energy was gone, and his metal skeleton threatened to pull him under the water. It was only the armbands that kept him afloat. But he was so tired.

Archie was vaguely aware of a noise approaching downriver.

A circle of light moved towards him—the police helicopter. Archie dragged the armbands off, dipped his head underwater, and allowed himself to sink, cutting off the noise of the helicopter's blades. Without the armbands, he dropped like a stone and soon found himself on the riverbed. The surface seemed so far above him, if it was even there. It was hard to tell in the murk of the Thames. He wanted to swim towards it, but he was so heavy and so cold. It might be easier to stay where he was.

He thought of Chloe. *She'll be so excited to meet me finally.*

With a burst of effort, Archie propelled himself from the river bed. After what seemed forever, he broke the surface and spat out a mouthful of water.

It took much of his energy to retrieve the armbands, more than he had to spare, but he forced them back on and fixed his sights on the far bank. Another fear quickly took hold—ahead was a

sheer unclimbable wall. He decided to ignore that detail for now. Maybe it would look different when he got closer.

The current was strong, and for every couple of feet he swam, he drifted a foot downstream. He repeatedly fought his way back and was getting nearer, but there was more distance than he had energy. He wiped a soggy paw across his eyes. It was too far.

The water level crept over his mouth, and an image appeared in his mind. It was Jack, his best and only friend. After his driving lesson, Jack, in a rare complimentary moment, said to him: 'Archie, sometimes you make me appreciate that we can do anything we put our minds to.'

He could do this. Archie centred his gaze on a spot on the far side and swam, drawing strength he didn't know he had. Finally, his paw touched a vertical wall of concrete. Archie drifted downstream with the current, and then he saw something. He let his paw trail along the slimy wall until he caught hold of a black shape. It was a chain with both ends attached near the top of the wall. The dip of the chain was low, almost touching the water. Archie had no idea why it was there, but it was a chance.

He wrapped the chain around his arm, took a moment and then pulled himself up. His head was barely out of the water when he fell back exhausted. Somehow, though, he kept hold of the chain. He just needed to rest.

After a couple of minutes, Archie started to feel sleepy—he had to move. With colossal effort, he pulled his body out of the water, waited a moment to allow some water to drain from his fur and then pulled himself up another foot. He continued in this fashion, climb and wait, climb and wait, until he somehow found himself at the top. He used the last of his energy to pull himself over and fell to the path where he froze more unsuspecting tourists, but he didn't care. He just wanted to get away, get home... get warm.

That's if he could stand.

Archie glanced at the human statues, and somehow, he forced himself upright. He staggered away until he was inside the neighbouring park and collapsed in some shrubs. He'd get dressed shortly, he told himself. But before he could do anything more, his vision faded to black, and he lost consciousness.

CHAPTER 15

CHLOE STOOD AT THE front room window, straining to see the helicopter that was flying around not far from their house. 'What do you think's happened?' she asked her mum. 'It's been flying around for hours.'

'Perhaps someone's gone missing,' Edith said. 'If it's anything serious, it'll be on the news.'

As the chopping sound of the helicopter's blades receded, Chloe sat back down.

'So, have you made any friends at school yet?' Edith asked.

Chloe shrugged.

'What does that mean?'

'I spoke to one girl, Annabelle. She's a bit moody, but she's quite funny.'

'Well, get to know her, and then you'll meet her friends as well.'

'Hmm,' Chloe said, not convinced.

'And if you prefer her friends, you can dump Annabelle and be friends with them instead.'

'Mum!'

'What? Is that wrong?'

'Yes, extremely!'

Edith smiled. 'I am joking.'

'Good!'

Edith shrugged. 'So, are you going to—'

CRASHHH

Chloe jumped and instinctively stepped towards her mum. 'What was that?'

Edith stared at the dining room door. 'Wait here.' She crept into the corridor, waited a few seconds, and then shouted. 'George, was that you?'

Chloe immediately decided to follow.

'No,' he shouted back from his bedroom.

Edith gently pushed the spare room door, flipped the light switch and tiptoed in with Chloe close behind. Archie was lying on the floor in a puddle of water. His fur and clothes were drenched. 'Archie! What the—'

She realised Chloe was behind her.

'Chloe, I told you to wait.'

'I want to see!'

Edith shook her head, walked to Archie, and knelt. She felt his fur. 'He's soaked. And what's happened to his ear? There's a hole going through it!'

'Really?' Chloe said as she joined her mum. 'Poor Archie... and he's wearing my old mask!' Chloe pulled the red superhero mask off Archie's head and studied it. 'This is so weird....'

'I think someone's playing a game with us.' She picked up Archie and sniffed his fur. 'He smells like seawater. Or worse.'

Chloe pressed her face to Archie's body. It wasn't that bad, but Mum was wrong. He didn't smell like seawater—that had a sweet, salty smell. This was different.

'This is so weird,' Edith said. 'I'm going to talk to George.' She stormed upstairs.

Chloe followed close behind, determined not to miss any clues. Edith knocked on George's door and threw it open.

George jumped and ripped his headphones off. 'Mum! You almost gave me a heart attack. Isn't there like a law or something against bursting into teenage boys' bedrooms?'

'Did you soak Archie?'

'What? I haven't left my room.'

Chloe felt he was telling the truth—after all, he wouldn't have left his room voluntarily.

'Chloe was with me, so I know it wasn't her,' Edith said.

'I've been playing my game,' George complained. 'Look!' He pointed at a timer at the top right of the screen.

Edith opened her mouth as if to argue, but there was nothing to say. She took Archie to the bathroom, where she and Chloe undressed him and stuck him under the shower.

'What on earth is going on?' she mumbled, more to herself than to Chloe, as she dried him with a towel.

Chloe racked her brain for answers, but nothing came. *What was going on?* She followed her mum downstairs to the spare room, where she laid Archie on a clean towel and left his shirt, braces, and striped trousers next to him.

Edith looked around. 'Was there a heater in here somewhere?'

Chloe nodded, went to a box in the corner of the room and dragged out an old electric fan heater from the junk. She put it down near Archie and plugged it in.

Edith leaned in, set the dial for one hour and flicked the switch. It rattled a bit, but it worked.

After that, they went to the kitchen, and Edith checked the kitchen door that led outside. It was locked as it should be. As an afterthought, she drew her face close to the glass and peered out. She let out a shriek of surprise.

'What!' Chloe cried, a little scared.

Edith recovered. 'It's nothing, just my reflection.'

Chloe breathed out. 'What's happening, Mum?' she asked as Edith checked another window.

Edith put her hand on Chloe's shoulder. 'I really don't know.'

After checking the house was secure, they returned to the dining room, where Edith collapsed in the armchair. Chloe sat on the sofa and watched her mum as she took out her mobile and started texting. Her hands shook as she typed, which was not a good sign. 'Who are you texting?'

Edith stared at her phone for a few seconds.

'I was going to text my sister, see if she's ever noticed anything strange happening here. But I'd only worry her.'

Chloe frowned. More stress would not help them get back to their proper home.

Edith put on a brave face. 'Let's find something to watch.'

Chloe would rather discover why Archie was wet but seeing how shaken up Mum looked, she decided TV was the better option. 'Okay.'

They watched TV, but Edith's eyes were glazed, her thoughts clearly elsewhere. Chloe knew how she felt. She could only think about Archie. Why did she feel like she'd frozen the other day? And why did her great-grandfather think Archie was special? And why was he soaking wet? And did George really write the note?

CHAPTER 16

AT ALMOST THREE IN the morning, Archie opened his eyes. He forgot where he was for a moment, but the chandelier above him confirmed he was back in the spare room. He was a mass of pain and exhaustion. Even his lungs hurt. He felt his chest. *Do I have lungs? It feels like I do.* He was too tired to think about such questions.

With extreme effort, he sat up and then slumped back down. He'd just close his eyes for a few more seconds and then try again.

Just before four, Archie woke for the second time. He slowly sat up. It hurt. He slumped over his hind paws and stared at the floor. And then he noticed something—he was naked. Again! He forced himself upright and slowly dressed.

Memories seeped back: He'd been to the Tower of London. There was a robot. Soldiers chased him and—oh! Archie turned to the window, shuffled across and pulled the curtain back. Beside the window in a pool of water was the rucksack containing the Crown Jewels.

Archie stared at the rucksack, dread gnawing at his insides. What if this didn't work? What if this had all been a spectacularly bad idea? He mopped the puddle under the window with the towel and then dried the jewels. Despite his exhaustion, he had to see it through.

He found some paper and wrote a simple line:

I said I would prove it. Archie x

Archie checked the way was clear, picked up the Crown Jewels, and began the climb to Chloe's bedroom.

CHAPTER 17

EDITH ROSE EARLY, MADE herself a cup of tea and some cereal, and took them into the front room. She switched on the morning news, lifted a spoon to her mouth, and stopped. There were police cars stationed outside the Tower of London. Something big had happened. A banner ran along the bottom of the screen. 'Breaking News—Crown Jewels stolen.'

'How?' Edith whispered and lowered her spoon.

A reporter stood outside the Tower of London, brushed hair out of her eyes and spoke to the camera. 'Last night, just after six, items from the Crown Jewels collection housed at the Tower of London were stolen. So far, we have not been told which items, and there has been no word on how the thief or thieves achieved this. We understand no one was hurt. The most pressing question is... *how*?'

Edith nodded in agreement.

'The jewels were kept in what is more or less a bank vault. They were in bombproof cabinets, under constant surveillance and protected by a heavily armed guard....'

Edith sat glued to the TV as her tea and breakfast went cold.

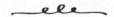

Chloe woke, stared at the ceiling for a minute and then lowered her gaze.

There was something on her chair.

She rubbed her eyes. *What is it? It looks like—*

Chloe sat up suddenly. 'No way!'

She swung her feet off the bed, dropped to the floor, and went to the chair.

'No....'

A gold sceptre lay across the seat. Chloe recognised it instantly and knew the huge jewel at one end was the world's largest colourless cut diamond. And it was in her bedroom. Next to the sceptre was a golden orb with a ring of gemstones and a cross. Beside it sat a crown set with precious jewels, including the Cullinan II diamond.

Chloe put a hand to her mouth. Her heart was racing, her mind a muddle. *How can the Crown Jewels be here? Are they real? It's not possible.* She looked away and then back, but the priceless treasure stubbornly remained.

She then noticed a folded note with her name printed in wobbly capitals. The letter scared her almost as much as the jewels, but she opened it anyway.

I said I would prove it. Archie x

Chloe dropped the note. This couldn't have been her brother. But what was the alternative? She nervously picked the crown up, placed it on her head and then gently took the sceptre in her other hand.

She stood opposite the wardrobe, which contained a full-length mirror and let her eyes wander over the treasures. 'I'm dreaming,' she whispered. Her reflection repeated the words.

Chloe had heard that you couldn't read things in a dream. Your brain turns the letters into nonsense. She selected a book from her bookcase and successfully read the title aloud. Did that mean she was awake, or maybe she was just wrong about not being able to read during a dream? It was hard to know.

There was a knock at the door. 'Chloe, you'll never guess what's happened,' Edith said from the other side of the door. She knocked again and let herself in.

Chloe turned. The Imperial State Crown slipped, and she grabbed it with her one free hand. The other still held the Sovereign Sceptre.

Edith entered. She took one look at her daughter wearing the stolen Imperial State Crown, and her skin turned an instant shade of grey. Then she opened her mouth and let out a high-pitched scream.

Chloe just stared at her mum. What was going on? Was any of this real?

Edith stopped and sucked in air. Her gaze drifted down her daughter's body to the Sovereign Sceptre, and she screamed again.

Chloe was confused. Her legs suddenly felt weak, and she sunk onto her bed.

Archie lay on the carpet in the spare room with his eyes shut. As Edith's scream echoed through the house, his eyes snapped open. He struggled to his feet and ran towards Chloe's room—something had freaked Edith out, and he could guess exactly what it might be.

As Archie passed the front room, he realised that The News was still on, and he stopped to watch for a few seconds, his heart sinking. It seemed he'd seriously underestimated how important the Crown Jewels were. *He was only borrowing them!*

He suddenly felt very awake.

Archie ran up to Chloe's room and burst through the door. Edith and Chloe instantly froze, and he took the opportunity to grab the crown from Chloe's head, the sceptre from her hand, and he recovered the golden orb from the chair.

He climbed onto Chloe's shoulder and heaved the Jewels onto the top of the wardrobe. Then he shoved a few toys in front, hiding the jewels. He dropped back onto the bed, grabbed the note and ran downstairs.

Thirty seconds later, he returned with Chloe's unfinished homemade Crown Jewels. He placed the cardboard crown on Chloe's head and the sceptre made from a cardboard tube and shiny wrapping paper in her hand.

Then he ran.

——*ele*——

Chloe and Edith emerged from their trance at the same time.

Edith was about to continue screaming when she looked back at Chloe and paused, staring at her in shock.

Chloe felt her head and then pulled the cardboard crown off. She blinked. *What?* She looked down at her hand, which held a cardboard staff wrapped in gold paper.

They both looked at each other.

'What happened?' Edith mumbled.

Chloe sat there in stunned silence.

'Were you just wearing—?' Edith's speech stumbled. Her mouth opened and shut a few more times, and she gave up trying to form words. 'I'm sorry for screaming,' she finally said. 'I thought... I thought you were wearing the Crown Jewels. The real ones. Maybe I should speak to a doctor.'

Chloe looked at the cardboard crown. *What is going on?*

'They've been stolen, you know.'

'What has?' Chloe asked, her mind a blur of impossible thoughts.

'The Crown Jewels.'

'Oh.'

'I need to sit down,' Edith said and left the room.

Chloe massaged her shoulder, aware of a slight pain that she could not explain. She noticed a dark brown hair under her fingers—darker than her own hair. She placed it on her bedside cabinet. And she'd frozen again, just like the man on the news. What was going on? She looked for the note, but it was gone.

Nothing made any sense.

CHAPTER 18

DETECTIVE MASTERS STOOD IN his hallway, chatting on the landline. 'Thank you, sir; you won't regret it.' With a smile, he replaced the phone. He was now part of the investigation into the theft of the Crown Jewels. Masters checked his tie in the hallway mirror and strolled from the house towards his unmarked police car.

He pulled up at the Tower of London, jumped out and introduced himself at the front gates. After inspecting his ID, a Yeoman Guard took him to the CCTV room. 'I'll wait for you here, detective,' he said and opened the door.

'Thank you,' Masters replied as he entered the small room. Banks of monitors showed every part of the Tower, although most cameras were in and around Jewel House.

A middle-aged woman sat at the monitors reviewing previous footage.

'Morning. I'm Detective Masters.'

She smiled. 'Good morning, detective.'

'So, what have we got?'

'A mystery,' she replied. She pointed to a screen and rewound the footage to just after six. 'Here, you can see the Crown Jeweller, Mr Pearson, arriving for the jewels' annual clean. Two soldiers remain outside. Two more escort him into Jewel House and open the vault doors. They remain on guard there whilst he works.'

She pressed a button, and the camera angle changed. 'Mr Pearson sets up his cleaning station. That takes a few minutes.' She forwarded the video. 'He removes the Coronation Regalia and is about to sit down. I'll pause it here.'

'Okay.'

'You'll note there's a stool there. The timestamp shows 18:06:24.'

Masters nodded.

She pressed play. The footage became snowy, and she forwarded through the next six minutes or so, at which point Mr Pearson reappeared and continued sitting. Only the stool was gone, and he fell to the floor. He jumped up and looked around, his face a picture of utter confusion. The Coronation Regalia he had been about to clean were gone.

'It would be funny if it weren't so weird,' she said and sniggered anyway. Her professional manner quickly returned under Masters' steely glare. 'It was the same situation with the soldiers outside—they're there, and then the footage turns snowy. Although you do see them a couple of times for a few seconds.'

Show me, please.

'Sure.'

Masters watched the entire footage. 'Strange. They seem spooked by something.'

'They do,' the operator agreed.

Masters slowly shook his head as he tried to make sense of it.

'The robot, Brad, put up a fight.'

'Brad?'

'Big Red Angry Droid,' she explained. 'We found a couple of laser burn marks. It fired at something or someone. I didn't even know it could do that. I thought it was just there to entertain our younger visitors. Regrettably, it's not fitted with any video recording equipment.'

'It's a puzzle,' Masters said. 'Could anyone have accessed this room and tampered with the footage?'

'Impossible. There are numerous safeguards. We also upload the footage remotely, so even if someone got in, it wouldn't do them any good as there's a backup off-site.'

'So, what are we saying here? The perpetrator stopped time?'

She shrugged. 'Well, time seems to have elapsed. We just haven't recorded it.'

'Intriguing. Obviously, we'll need copies of all this.'

'Already sent, on the understanding that the footage is for key personnel's eyes only,' she said sternly.

'Understood. And did the thief or thieves leave anything behind?'

'Yes, it's with your crime scene investigators.'

'I haven't checked in with them yet. What did they find?'

'I understand there were two items of interest, a note which says—and you won't believe this—just borrowed.'

'Okay...,' Masters said.

'Yep. And the robot had a handful of hair.'

Masters pondered his next question. 'Anything unusual about the hair?'

'They didn't tell me, sorry. But I understand there was plenty of it. I'm sure they'll let you have a sample.'

'Do you have any thoughts on what happened?' Masters asked.

'Not a clue.'

'Okay. I guess I should speak to the soldiers who were on duty and then look at the crime scene. Thanks for your time.'

'You're welcome.' She returned to the monitors as Masters left.

The guard led him to the Yeoman Warders Club, also known as The Keys. They entered through a wooden door set under a stone arch in the castle wall. The exclusive pub existed for the enjoyment of the men and women who worked and lived on the grounds.

Other than the executioner's axe displayed on one wall and some ancient memorabilia, the club looked like any other. The Yeoman Guard pointed to four sombre-looking soldiers. Two sat at the end of a long red leather bench, and two opposite on leather chairs. A long, dark wood table ran between them.

'The two on the chairs were stationed outside,' the Yeoman Guard said.

'Thanks.'

Masters walked over and took a seat. 'Good morning, I'm Detective Eddie Masters. Thanks for taking the time to speak to me.'

They nodded.

He turned to the first two on chairs. 'After escorting Mr Pearson to Jewel House, I understand you remained on guard outside.'

'That's right,' the older of the two replied.

The other mumbled in agreement.

'I'll start with the obvious,' Masters said. 'How did the thief or thieves get past you?'

The men shuffled uncomfortably. The older man wasn't in the best of moods, so Masters wasn't expecting much from him, but he was first to speak.

'We know what we're doing. We stood there, weapons ready, and then... time stopped. I know that sounds crazy, but that's what happened. If anyone says any different, I'll be happy to convince them.'

The man next to him nodded in agreement. 'This theft was impossible.'

'And yet it happened,' Masters said. 'You saw nothing at all? However fleeting?'

Both hesitated but shook their heads.

Masters nodded but kept eye contact. 'The footage lasts a little over six minutes, mostly just white noise, but there are a couple of moments when you appear. You look spooked by something.'

'True enough,' the old soldier said. 'But then, straight away, we were out again. I don't know what to tell you.'

The other soldiers nodded.

Masters felt they might be holding back but didn't doubt they were baffled.

He turned his attention to the other two. 'You were on the inside, I believe. What did you see?'

The men looked at each other before one spoke. 'The same. We were at the vault doors, and then the jewels were gone. During the theft, I was not conscious. That's all I can tell you.'

'Same for you?' he asked the other soldier on the bench.

The man took a moment to answer. 'Yes. There was nothing we could have done.' He let out a frustrated sigh. 'The public won't believe that, though, will they?'

Masters did his best to appear positive. 'I'm sure you have the public's trust. It would, of course, be better if we could offer an explanation.'

The men were quiet.

'Do your lot have any ideas?' one man asked Masters.

'There was a story in the paper a couple of days ago, something about people losing time.' Masters nodded towards the Thames. 'Happened just over the river. I realise it's bizarre, but some thought they saw a toy bear or puppet before it happened. Did you see anything that you can't explain?'

The men looked at each other nervously before mumbling 'no' or shaking their heads. Masters studied them. There was something they weren't saying. Although if it was like the event at Potters Fields, that was understandable. Maybe they'd have more to say when they were alone.

Masters gave them each a card with his contact details. 'If you think of anything, please let me know. And I mean anything, no matter how insane it sounds.'

He continued with his enquiries. The heavily guarded crime scene didn't add much. He learnt that the thief or thieves wrote the note on printer paper but left no fingerprints. Crime scene investigators gave him a few of the hairs they'd recovered from the robot, which they placed in a small, clear plastic bag. The hairs looked manufactured rather than organic, so they weren't human. It was all very odd.

Masters returned to the police station and sat at his desk. The only real clue was the people losing time at Potters Fields—it was too similar to the guards' recollection of events at the Tower to be a coincidence. He turned on his PC, entered his password, and loaded up a search engine. He typed *Who made the Amazing Archie* and pressed enter.

The results were not quite what he wanted. He was interested in who made the bear, not who made the TV show, but there was a number for the company responsible, and he thought it was worth a call. After fifteen minutes of being passed around and put on hold, they found him a number for an employee who worked on the show.

Masters dialled the number and waited.

An elderly man answered. 'Hello?'

Masters sat up straight. 'Hi, is that Harold Wyatt?'

'That's me. Who's calling?'

'My name's Detective Eddie Masters. I'm hoping you can help me with a few questions.'

'Whatever's happened, it wasn't me,' the old man said and laughed until he broke into a coughing fit.

'Haha, I'm sure it wasn't. You worked on The Amazing Archie show, is that correct?'

'You're going back, but yes, I did. I was only a lad—a runner. I'd do whatever was needed.'

'Do you know where Archie came from? As in, who made him?'

'It was a local company, something Toys. Tiny Toys, that was it. Stupid name. I mean, Archie must have been nearly four feet tall. That all you need?'

Masters picked a pen up and rolled it through his fingers. 'Do you know if they made more than one Archie toy?'

'Oh yes, hundreds. Possibly thousands. He was big business back then. Kids loved him.'

Masters frowned. 'Okay, thanks for your help. By the way, do you have any idea what happened to Archie?'

'Nah, I left before the end.'

'Okay, thanks,' Master said. He ended the call and dropped the pen. He sat back for a moment and then found the number for Tiny Toys. To his surprise, they were still in business.

After a quick call, Masters picked up his jacket and headed off.

'Got a lead, Eddie?' a police officer asked.

'Perhaps.'

'Where you off to?'

'To see a company called Tiny Toys.'

'Shouldn't you save your hobbies for your own time, Sir?' an officer with slicked-back blond hair asked.

Masters turned to PC John Leary. He was young and a little too full of himself for his liking.

'Is that where criminals hang out, sir?' Leary continued.

Masters gave him a quick smile and left.

Tiny Toys was a half-hour drive. It gave him a chance to think about things.

By the time he arrived, he was less optimistic about finding out anything useful. What could a toy bear have to do with any of this?

Masters rang the bell at Tiny Toys' entrance. 'Hi, Detective Eddie Masters. I called a half-hour ago.' The receptionist buzzed him through and showed him to a plush office. A smartly dressed middle-aged man with a few wisps of hair combed over his head asked him to take a seat opposite his desk.

'Thanks for seeing me,' Masters said.

The man nodded. 'You have some hair you want me to view?'

'Yes, please.' Masters took his wallet out and removed the clear bag. 'I understand you made teddy bears that looked like Archie?'

The man eyed the bag with interest. 'That's right. Of course, my dad was running things in those days, but I know a bit about it.'

Masters passed over the little bag with the hairs. 'Can you tell me if these were used in your company's Archie toys?'

The man located a large book, which included a picture of every bear the company had made, and a sample of the materials used. He placed the hairs on the book and pulled a small microscope from a drawer.

The man put his eye to the eyepiece and adjusted the magnification. His eyebrows lifted towards the top of his head, and he smiled.

'What?' Masters asked.

'It's not one of the Archie bears.'

'Oh,' Masters said, a little disappointed. He sunk back into his chair. 'Shame.'

The man handed the bag back. 'It's not one of them. It's the original. You see, we dyed his hair a little darker than usual. It was better for the camera. What you have there is hair from the original Archie. I must say I'm extremely curious where you found these.'

Masters sat up and leaned in. 'You're sure?'

'The hair we used had a specific weave. Of course, it's possible that someone else used the same hair for some reason and dyed it the same colour, but unlikely.'

'Now that is interesting.'

The man looked thoughtful. 'Any idea where Archie is?'

Masters shook his head. 'That's what I was going to ask you. Any theories?'

'Only the one. Archie was a bit of a celebrity here, and people talk. Or at least they did. The most likely scenario is that Jack Goodman took him. He worked on the show—one of the animators. It seems he formed an attachment to him. He died in the sixties, but maybe his family can help. Although I suspect they'd be reluctant to admit hanging on to stolen property.'

'That's helpful. Thanks.' Masters said.

'May I ask why the enquiries?'

Masters paused. 'We found the hairs at a crime scene.'

'How odd.'

Masters watched his reaction, but it seemed entirely normal. He doubted he knew anything. 'It is. I'm afraid I can't say any more than that but thank you for your help.'

The man nodded. 'Well, if you find him, please let us know.'

Masters nodded back. 'We will.'

CHAPTER 19

CHLOE SAT IN HER maths lesson, staring out of the window. The events of the morning had left her questioning her sanity. She *had been* wearing the Crown Jewels, she knew it.

'Chloe, would you care to answer?'

Chloe jumped.

'Is my lesson boring you?'

'No, sir. I err—I was just thinking about my mum. She was feeling unwell this morning.' It was not entirely a lie and better than talking about why she was really distracted.

'Okay,' her teacher said and swiftly moved on. 'I asked you to calculate nineteen multiplied by seventeen, and no calculators, please. Use your head. I appreciate that's a large number, but I'll explain a simple way to—'

Chloe took a second, multiplied seventeen by ten to get a hundred and seventy, then doubled it and subtracted seventeen.

'Three hundred and twenty-three, sir.'

The teacher stopped talking. He'd lost his flow. 'Good,' he said reluctantly and turned to a sleepy-looking boy. 'Patrick, how did Chloe work that out?'

'She's clever, sir.'

'That may be true, but not really the answer I was looking for. Anyone else?'

Chloe tuned out again. *I know the jewels were real. I didn't imagine them.*

The rest of the day dragged. Chloe enjoyed learning, but not today.

After a quiet journey back and an equally quiet dinner—she still refused to speak to George—Chloe was relieved to go to her room. She sat on the edge of her bed and remembered the hair from earlier. It was a couple of centimetres, darkish brown and thicker than a human hair. It could be one of Archie's, but why was it on her shoulder? On her nightdress? She'd never even held Archie while wearing her nightdress.

Chloe pulled a silver filigree locket from her drawer, opened its glass window and placed the hair inside. The metalwork was fine enough that she doubted the hair would escape through the tiny holes.

Her shoulder was still sore as though something heavy had pressed down on it... or trodden on her. As she massaged it, she glanced up at her wardrobe. The toys and junk piled on top looked different somehow. It was too suspicious to ignore.

She got up and stood on the wooden frame at the end of her bed to reach the top of her wardrobe. After moving a few items aside, the light caught something. Chloe gasped and dropped back down. Her heart raced, pumping blood through her veins at unnatural speed.

With some effort, she slowed her breathing just like she'd seen her mother do when she was panicky. Once her heartbeat felt more like a human's and less like a hummingbird's, she climbed back up on the bed frame and reached for the top of the wardrobe again

Chloe's hand found some sort of cross. 'No, no, no...' she mumbled. It was hard to see from her angle, but once she'd withdrawn the item, there was no doubt. It was the Sovereign Sceptre—held by generations of kings and queens, and now her. She brought the enormous diamond to eye level. It was beautiful, but it made her feel sick. A shudder racked her body, and she dropped the sceptre onto the bed.

She stared at it, willing it to go away, but it didn't. It just lay there glittering expensively. Even worse, she knew there was more to find.

She took a deep breath, stood on tiptoes, reached to the back of the wardrobe, and withdrew the Sovereign Orb, quickly followed by the magnificent Imperial State Crown. She climbed down and placed them next to the sceptre.

Chloe stared at her bed. How was this possible? How could the Crown Jewels be on her bed?

She took a step back and looked at herself in her wardrobe mirror. She looked real, nothing like a dream version of herself. This was really happening.

Her instinct was to tell her mum, but then she remembered her screams the first time she'd seen the jewels. And if Mum's stress levels didn't improve, their life would never return to normal, and she'd never see her friends again.

She paced up and down her room. As the only adult in the house, her mum would be the prime suspect. If Mum handed them in, which Chloe felt was highly likely, would the police believe she was innocent? Of course not. They'd lock her up, and then she and George would have to live with strangers, or they'd be sent to a children's home. Or maybe if you were found guilty of stealing from the King, you just mysteriously disappeared?

'Stop!' she cried aloud as her thoughts became too much. Every angle ended badly. There was only one answer—return the Crown Jewels without anyone knowing.

She remembered the note signed 'Archie.' The logical explanation was that George had written it—the same as the last one. But surely he couldn't have stolen the Crown Jewels, could he?

She picked the locket up again and slipped it over her neck, deciding to compare the hair inside to Archie's hair. First, she returned the Crown Jewels to the top of her wardrobe and arranged her toys in front of them.

She tramped downstairs and stopped at George's bedroom door—it couldn't hurt to ask a couple of questions, could it? She raised her fist, ready to knock, but paused. If he denied leaving the note, what would she say?

She knocked on the door anyway. 'Can I come in?'

'No,' George shouted back.

Chloe stood there, pondering what to do next. She could barge in and demand answers. Or maybe being super nice would get better results. But even if he had written the note, he couldn't have been responsible for the theft unless he was a secret criminal genius, able to sneak past trained soldiers. It seemed unlikely.

'Okay,' she said to the closed door. She'd decided he couldn't be involved and continued downstairs.

A few seconds later, George's door opened and quickly closed again.

On her way past the front room, she peeked in. Edith was lying on the couch watching TV, although it looked like she might have dozed off.

Chloe eased open the spare room door. Archie was sitting in front of his crate. She stared at him for a moment, confused. Had Mum moved and dressed him? She knelt opposite him but already doubted herself. How could a puppet be involved in the theft of the Crown Jewels? She bit her lip. This was stupid. But she was a logical girl, and the evidence pointed in this direction.

'Was it you, Archie?'

Archie didn't move.

'The Jewels. Did you—'

This was insane. She stood up to leave.

Archie looked up.

For a moment, nothing made any sense.

Chloe half choked, half screamed. She tried to stand and fell backwards. She clamped a hand across her mouth and pushed herself along the floor, away from Archie.

'You okay, Chloe?' Edith shouted.

Chloe stared at Archie.

Archie looked back at her in disbelief. 'You can see me?'

Chloe backed up further as she heard Archie's gruff but well-spoken voice. She nodded, her hand still clamped over her mouth.

There was movement in the front room, so she forced herself to call back. 'I'm fine, Mum. Just a spider.'

'Okay,' Edith replied, sounding relieved. She wasn't keen on spiders, so Chloe knew she wouldn't come to investigate.

'How is this possible?' Chloe whispered.

Archie shuffled forward but stopped when he saw the fear on Chloe's face. 'I can't believe you can see me. You wanted the Crown Jewels, and I thought that if I got them for you, you'd realise I was alive. Or at least I hoped....'

'What?'

'The Crown Jewels. I thought that....'

Chloe's mind felt as though it had collapsed in on itself. As it unfolded, Archie's words gradually made some sort of sense, but it was impossible... wasn't it? She was pretty sure she wasn't asleep. And this felt real unless, of course, she'd unexpectedly gone mad. She might as well go with it.

'The Crown Jewels... when did I say I wanted the Crown Jewels?'

'You were talking to your mum about your school project. You wanted the real ones to copy.'

Chloe gave her skin a fierce pinch. Archie was still there. 'I was joking,' Chloe said. 'Obviously.'

'Well, yes, perhaps... but the point was, if it wasn't George or your mum, then who's left? I hoped you'd realise my note had to be true.'

Chloe's mouth hung open, and she realised she was drooling. She wiped her mouth with her sleeve. This couldn't be real. Maybe she really did have some bizarre medical condition.

Archie looked at her with wide eyes. 'It seemed the only way to prove I'm alive. And it worked!'

She jumped when he spoke. 'But you're not real!'

'What do you mean?' Archie asked.

'I mean, you're a toy or a puppet. Toys don't talk!'

'I didn't, and then one day I did,' Archie said. 'Your great grandfather suggested that my admirers' wishes came true. I was a TV star, you see, with fans worldwide.'

Archie looked quite proud when he said this, which Chloe found rather irritating. She opened her mouth, but no words came out. She took a breath and tried again. 'Wishes don't come true.'

Archie shrugged. 'Mine has.' He smiled at Chloe.

A barrage of thoughts and rationalisations raced through her brain, but in the end, Archie was still there, and she had to accept that this was real.

'So, you stole the Crown Jewels to get my attention?'

'Borrowed, but yes,' Archie replied.

Chloe got to her feet. 'You terrorised my family.'

'What?' Archie's mouth flattened.

Chloe took a step closer. 'My mum is losing her mind.'

'I just wanted company!'

Her hands became fists. 'I thought I was going mad!'

Archie looked up at her. 'But now you know!'

She leaned towards him, her anger building. 'I accused my brother of lying to me, and I haven't spoken to him since!'

Archie looked like he was near tears. 'I'm sorry.'

'Oh, and you STOLE the Crown Jewels!'

'I had to,' Archie pleaded. 'It was the only way you'd realise the truth.'

'Chloe, what are you shouting at?' Edith called from the front room.

Chloe heard her mom get up and approach. 'I should turn you in now.'

Archie's voice cracked. 'You can't imagine what it's like to have no one, to be completely and utterly alone.'

'So, you steal and hurt people to get what you want?'

'I....' Archie stuttered as he searched for the right words.

Edith opened the door. 'Chloe, what's going—'

Edith saw Archie and froze.

Chloe gasped in horror. For a moment, it felt like her heart had forgotten to beat. After a few seconds, she closed her mouth and walked up to her mother. 'What—how?'

Archie frowned. 'I don't know. It just happens. I hate it.'

She touched her mum's cheek. There was nothing, no movement, no awareness. 'Great, now she'll really lose it.'

'It'll be okay,' Archie said.

She was now too angry to be scared. 'No. It won't!'

'I can go into a sort of hibernation. It's like shutting myself down.'

Chloe watched as Archie's eyes dimmed, and his head fell. She turned back to her mum and waited.

After a couple of minutes, Edith returned to life. She looked confused.

'Are you okay, Mum?' Chloe asked.

'What? I don't know. Chloe, who were you talking to?'

'No one, just err—acting out a story.'

'Oh.' But she wasn't convinced. 'What's it about?'

Chloe looked at Archie's slumped form and felt conflicted between amazement and anger. Either way, she had to protect her mum from the truth. 'It's about someone who wants to be my friend, but they really only care about themselves.'

'It sounds very grown-up,' Edith said.

'I don't think I'll finish it. I don't like the character.' Chloe walked to the door. She held it open for her mum.

Edith glanced at Archie. 'Did you dress him?'

'Oh, err, yes,' Chloe lied.

Edith didn't speak for a moment.

'Mum?' Chloe said.

'Sorry, yes, I'm coming.'

Edith passed through into the hallway. Chloe followed and pulled the door shut behind her.

'Tea?' Chloe asked her mum.

Edith looked at her suspiciously. 'Okay...'

Chloe smiled as she headed for the kitchen, but despite her calm exterior, her brain was screaming at her. *There's a living, talking toy bear in the spare room. Whatever it is, it stole the Crown Jewels. My life is over.*

Later that evening, Chloe returned to her bedroom, put her nightie on, and took off her locket. She wasn't tired, but she hoped sleep would solve her problems. Whenever her thoughts turned to Archie, she didn't know whether to scream with anger or cry with wonder. If Archie was real—and the evidence suggested he was—, then he was probably the most incredible being alive. And that scared her almost as much as the Crown Jewels. If people learnt of Archie, there would be chaos. Everyone would want to meet him—to know how he worked or to possess him.

Chloe tried to sleep, but having half a billion pounds of stolen jewels and a talking toy bear in the house would've played on anyone's mind. The outlines of a few soft toys in her bedroom also bothered her, so she threw a spare blanket over them. The lumpy silhouette wasn't much better.

Eventually, sleep found her, as did dreams of police and prisons, helicopters, executions, and talking toys who schemed behind your back.

CHAPTER 20

DETECTIVE EDDIE MASTERS WOKE early, keen to find the thieves who'd stolen the Crown Jewels. After his morning shower, he rustled up an omelette and wolfed it down. The first step of today's investigation was clear: A robot charged with protecting the jewels had a fistful of hair from the original Archie, so the bear must have been there when the thieves stole the jewels. If he found Archie, he'd likely find the criminals or at least a further clue.

He finished his breakfast and washed up. On the way past the hallway mirror, he stopped to check his appearance. 'Watch out, thieves, I'm coming for you.'

Masters grabbed his jacket, left the house, and climbed into his car. He drove away, humming a happy tune as he headed for work.

At the police station, Masters navigated a few twisting corridors and walked into an open-plan office, greeting colleagues as he passed. The office was busier than he expected. The boss must have called in the others early—after all, he wasn't the only police officer on the case.

'Where are you going today, Eddie, *Toys r Us*?' an officer joked.

'You won't be laughing when I catch the thieves.'

PC John Leary couldn't help but join in. 'Who do you think stole the jewels, then? Winnie the Pooh or Paddington?'

Masters shook his head.

'Maybe Ken and Barbie were in on it?' Leary added.

Masters gave a false smile. 'Hilarious. You know, if you're not busy, you could get the coffees in. And I expect your colleagues would appreciate a pastry of some sort. There's a nice little bakery on the corner of—'

Leary put his head down. 'I'm swamped, sir.'

'Shame,' Masters said as he sat and logged on to his computer. There was one name to go on—Jack Goodman, the man accused of taking the original Archie. After interrogating his computer for half an hour, Masters discovered that Jack had two granddaughters, Carole Webb and Edith Moran.

'Carole and Edith,' he said, stroking his chin, 'let's see what you know.' Now he just needed their contact details. With the police resources available, that wouldn't take long. He was already one step closer.

CHAPTER 21

EDITH FINISHED HER CEREAL and chucked the bowl in the sink. She went to the spare room, paused, and then eased the door open. A few seconds passed before she stepped inside.

The room looked normal, and Archie was in his box. Edith cautiously advanced, took a breath and bent down to lift the casket. It was heavy and awkward, so it took her a moment to manoeuvre it into a more comfortable position. She headed for the stairs, heaved Archie's box up both flights, and collapsed on the top floor landing. She caught her breath, stretched her aching back and then pulled down the attic ladder. Taking it slowly, she wrestled Archie's crate up the ladder and into the roof space.

The attic was overflowing with stuff. Her sister Carole had spent a fortune on equipment for various short-lived hobbies: Aerial photography, scuba diving, tennis, art, astronomy and so on. She would buy the best equipment in a rush of enthusiasm and then decide she didn't have time to pursue her new interest. Edith tutted at the discarded boxes.

She manoeuvred Archie's casket to the back and set him down. 'Sorry, Archie.' After a last look, she climbed back down the ladder and then pushed it back up the runners into its space. After closing the hatch, she walked down the hall.

Her step seemed just a little lighter.

Chloe woke from a difficult night, and a barrage of memories flooded to the surface. *The Crown Jewels are on top of your wardrobe. Archie can talk. George didn't write the note, and we're all going to prison.* She buried her head into her pillow, but you can't bury your thoughts, and returning to sleep didn't seem an option for her over-busy brain.

She climbed onto her bed frame and, with a stretch, pushed the front layer of toys on top of the wardrobe to one side. A gleaming diamond, bigger than her fist, winked at her. She'd returned them to the top of the wardrobe yesterday; unfortunately, they were still there. She hadn't imagined it.

Chloe sunk back down, and the sick feeling returned. At least she now understood why her great-grandfather had thought Archie was special. Archie's troubles were also nagging at her, but he'd put her entire family at serious risk just to make a point. He didn't deserve her pity, even though having a talking bear as a friend would be kind of cool.

Chloe got up and dragged on her school uniform. She couldn't see how she was supposed to learn with everything that was going on in her head, but she didn't get a say on the matter.

George stepped out as she neared his door on the way to the bathroom, and the atmosphere instantly became awkward.

'Morning, George,' Chloe said.

George ignored her and turned to go to the bathroom.

Chloe felt a sudden and overriding urge to apologise, as objectionable as the idea was. 'George...'

He spun. 'What?'

Chloe grimaced. She fiddled with her school skirt. 'I'm sorry about the note. I know now that you didn't write it.'

'What do you mean *now*?'

'It's complicated.'

'It's not complicated. Either you wrote it, or Mum did. And I doubt it was Mum.'

'There is a third option.'

George sighed loudly. 'Tell the truth or leave me alone.'

Chloe hesitated. She was scared that George would tell Mum every-thing, and she'd then get herself arrested. 'It's not that simple.'

'Fine. Never bother me again.'

George opened the bathroom door.

Chloe panicked. She couldn't handle arguing with George on top of everything else. 'Mum didn't write the note.'

'I know.'

'Before I can tell you any more, I need to show you something. But you need to promise it stays between us.'

'How can I promise that when I don't know what you're talking about?'

Chloe inwardly screamed, turned, and walked away. She didn't need him.

'Okay, fine. I promise,' George said at last.

Chloe turned back. 'Really?'

'I said it, didn't I?'

She stared at him. 'It's in my bedroom.'

After a moment, she turned and walked away.

George sighed but followed.

CHAPTER 22

MASTERS SAT BACK IN his chair and smiled. He'd found Edith's sister, Carole, on the internet. It hadn't taken long to establish that she was working abroad, so she was unlikely to have had anything to do with the heist. He would concentrate on Edith for now. He called her house number, planning to put the phone down if she answered, but the line was dead.

After a search on Edith's address, Masters found that her property was registered with a letting company. He phoned them and discovered that Edith was no longer living there. Masters pondered whether there was a connection—older sister abroad, younger sister moved out. Could Edith be staying at her sister's house while she was away? It wouldn't hurt to check.

As the house was close, he decided against phoning. Why risk alerting her when he could be there in minutes? He snatched his jacket from the back of the chair and headed off.

PC Leary looked up and was about to say something which no doubt would have been terribly amusing, but he seemed to think better of it.

'Cinnamon Swirl,' Masters said.

PC Leary gave Masters a confused look.

'You were about to ask me what pastry I'd like, weren't you?'

'Me, sir? No, sir.'

Masters left and smiled to himself.

CHAPTER 23

CHLOE PUT HER HAND on the doorknob and paused. She turned to George. 'Did you hear that the Crown Jewels have been stolen?'

'Of course,' George replied. 'I do live on this planet.'

She looked him straight in the eyes. 'They're in my bedroom.'

George laughed. 'Course they are.' Shaking his head, he followed her in.

Chloe jumped on her bed, climbed onto the frame and stretched for the back of her wardrobe. She turned to George. 'Come closer.'

George sighed but shuffled nearer.

'Take this for me,' Chloe said.

Chloe withdrew the Sovereign Sceptre from the top of her wardrobe and passed it to George, gold rod first. 'Careful, the diamond is worth four hundred million pounds.'

George's mouth dropped. He shook as he took it and brought the diamond to his face. 'Holy—'

'And this.' Chloe passed him the golden orb.

George lowered the sceptre to the bed, unhinged his fingers, and took the orb.

'Stop shaking,' Chloe urged. 'You'll drop it.'

George placed the orb on the bed.

'Chloe, what's... what's going on?'

'One more thing,' she said and rummaged around until she found the Imperial State Crown.

George backed away. 'I'm not touching that.'

'It's the sceptre you should be worried about.' She climbed down and laid the crown beside the sceptre and orb.

George stared at the bed as though in a trance.

'Are these... real?'

'Look at them. Of course, they're real.'

George turned a sickly shade of white. 'How?' he asked.

Chloe took a moment. 'It was Archie.'

'The teddy bear?'

'Puppet, but yeah.'

'The teddy bear stole the Crown Jewels? Don't be ridiculous.'

Chloe sighed. 'I'll show you. Follow me.'

George was in such a state of shock that he obeyed without argument.

Chloe stopped and turned to him. 'Remember, you promised me. You can't tell Mum about the jewels. She'll hand them in and end up in prison.'

George nodded numbly and followed her to Archie's room. They entered, and Chloe looked around. 'He's gone!' She turned back to the door. 'Mum!' she shouted. 'Where's Archie?'

Edith joined them. 'I'm sorry, but things have been weird since I got him out. I need time to think. For the sake of my sanity.'

'But Mum, I need him!' Chloe begged.

Edith ignored her, distracted by the sight of George swaying in the doorway. 'Are you okay, George? You look pasty.'

George steadied himself with a hand on the door frame. 'I don't feel too good.'

Edith placed a hand on his back and directed him through the door. 'Go back to bed. I'll let the school know.'

George didn't even answer. He left the room and trudged down the hall like a zombie.

'Can I see Archie, just for a minute, please?' Chloe begged.

'No,' Edith said. 'We'll talk about him when you get home.'

Chloe's face crumpled with frustration. 'Thanks for lying to me. Thanks a lot.'

'I'm sorry, Chloe, it's not that simple.'

'Yes, it is. You said your grandad would want me to look after him. You lied.' Chloe turned and stormed up the stairs.

Edith shouted after her. 'Chloe, don't talk to me like that.'

Chloe didn't answer. She had an idea. It was deceitful, and she knew she would feel guilty about it later, but she had no choice. She had to find Archie, and in order to do that, she needed her mum safely out of the way.

Five minutes later, the retching sounds coming from behind the bathroom door brought Edith running up the stairs, just as Chloe had hoped.

Edith knocked on the bathroom door. 'Is that you, Chloe?'

'Yes,' Chloe answered weakly and pulled the toilet chain.

'Are you okay?'

'I'm sick.'

'Oh,' Edith said. 'You too?'

'I'm sorry I was rude to you,' Chloe said. 'Can you get me something to settle my stomach, please?'

'I'll see what we've got.'

Edith entered the bathroom, avoiding Chloe, who was kneeling on the floor with her head over the toilet. She opened the bathroom medicine cabinet and began to rummage, shaking her head as she checked through the names on the boxes and packets. 'We haven't got anything, dear.'

'Please,' Chloe whined.

'I'll have to go out; will you be okay for thirty minutes or so? There's bound to be a queue.'

'Yes,' Chloe said. 'Hurry.'

'Okay, I'm going.'

Chloe looked down at the stomach remedy clutched in her fist, which she had removed from the medicine cabinet. It felt awful tricking Mum like this, but these were emergency circumstances.

She waited until she heard the front door open and shut and then ran from the bathroom to George's room. She pounded on his door and barged inside. 'George, we've got about thirty minutes before Mum's back.'

'I'm not well,' George said. 'Go away.'

'You're fine. I want you to meet Archie, and then you can do what you like.'

'No.'

'Are you scared?' Chloe asked. 'You are, aren't you? You're scared I'm telling you the truth. My big brother is a wimp—'

'I know what you're doing,' George said.

'How embarrassing, scared of a toy bear. Just wait—'

'A toy bear cannot do anything. It's just material and stuffing,' George snapped back.

'Then who stole the Crown Jewels? Do you think I sneaked past armed soldiers, opened bomb-proof cabinets, and then made it back with the jewels without anyone noticing?'

George glared back. 'Well, I know who *didn't* steal them, but I'll come just to shut you up.'

They checked each room until only one possibility remained—the attic.

'Go on, you're taller than me,' Chloe said.

George was reluctant, but he pulled down the hatch and ladder.

'After you,' Chloe said.

'Whatever.'

George climbed the steps and entered the attic, Chloe following behind him. He pulled on a chord, and a dim bulb lit the crowded space. In the far corner, Chloe could make out Archie's enclosure.

She stepped in front of George, walked up to Archie, and opened the barred door. The thought of talking to him suddenly seemed stupid, especially with George watching.

George smiled. 'Go on then.'

There was a nasty, amused tone to George's voice that Chloe did not enjoy. He'd be acting differently in a moment, though. She knelt opposite Archie's crate. 'Archie, we need to talk.'

For the tiniest second, Chloe was sure she saw the corners of Archie's mouth twisting up into a smile.

And in the next moment, she felt herself coming round, George shaking his head beside her as he did the same. They must have frozen.

'It happened again, didn't it?' Chloe moaned. 'Why? Why did it happen again?'

'Nothing happened, Chloe. I knew it wouldn't.'

'Nothing happened!' Chloe wanted to scream. 'We both froze. Do you call that nothing!'

'I'm not sure... but I know your stupid bear didn't come to life. You're so pathetic.'

DING DONG.

Chloe jumped. 'Who's that?'

'Sorry, I can't see through walls,' George replied.

'It can't be Mum. She only left five minutes ago.'

'Maybe, she forgot her keys,' George said.

Chloe growled and climbed down the ladder.

'Wait up,' George shouted and clambered down after her.

He shoved the ladder back and closed the hatch before running after Chloe.

Chloe made it to the front door first and pulled it open.

A man in his early forties, dressed in a suit, was standing at the door. He looked important. The man pulled out a badge from his wallet. 'Good morning. I'm Detective Masters. Is your mum or dad home?'

For a moment, Chloe just stood there with her mouth open, and George was no use. He looked like he'd seen the devil. 'Dad doesn't live here. And Mum's gone to the pharmacy; she'll be back in about half an hour. I can get her to call you.'

'Are you two okay? You look a little off.'

'We're not well,' they said in unison.

Masters looked them over. 'Oh dear. Well, maybe I could come in and wait?'

Chloe's jaw dropped. 'We're not allowed to invite in strangers.'

'I'm a policeman,' Masters replied, once again brandishing his badge.

Chloe looked at the badge. 'It could be fake.'

'Very wise,' Masters agreed. 'Which way is the chemist?'

Chloe pointed up the road.

'Oh, one more thing....'

Chloe felt her stomach turn. *What was he going to ask?*

'Is your mum's name Edith Moran?'

'Yes...'

'Okay, thanks. I'll wait in my car for her to return.' He indicated the vehicle parked over the road.

Chloe nodded. 'Okay.' She shut the door in his face, ran into the front room with George following and watched Masters go to his car. 'What are we going to do?'

'We?' George said. 'I didn't steal them.'

'And do you think I did?'

George shrugged.

She moved towards George. 'Do you think Mum stole them?'

'Of course not.'

The tendons in her neck stood out. 'Then who, George? Who stole the Crown Jewels?'

George backed away. 'We need to let Mum know what's going on. I'll call her.'

'Wait!' Chloe cried.

'No,' George said as he walked up the hallway. He picked up the house phone. Edith's mobile number was on a small piece of card by the phone.

George began pressing buttons.

Chloe ripped the telephone cable out from the wall socket.

'What did you do that for!' George shouted. 'We need help!'

Chloe held the telephone cable away from George. 'You promised me! And who will the police think took the jewels? A twelve-year-old, a fourteen-year-old, a puppet or Mum?'

George didn't answer.

'If you tell her, she'll hand them in and be arrested!'

George banged the phone down.

'She's already a nervous wreck,' Chloe said.

'What do you mean?'

Chloe shook her head, frustrated by her brother's lack of awareness. 'If you spent a bit less time online and a bit more time with your family, then you'd know.'

George scowled. 'Well, it wasn't Archie.'

'Yes, it was. Have you seen the news lately? People freezing, saying they lost time. Some even remember seeing a bear. It was Archie.'

'You're insane,' George said and stomped off towards his bedroom.

'Where are you going!' Chloe shouted.

'I need to think. Alone!'

CHAPTER 24

CHLOE RAN TO HER bedroom to check if the jewels were there. Standing on the bed frame, she pushed aside the toys and blinked as light from the window hit the diamond. Chloe groaned and fell to the bed. But what did she expect? If this were a dream, she would have woken by now. And the policeman waiting outside seemed frighteningly real.

She considered her options.

She could just tell the truth—Archie stole the jewels. They wouldn't believe her and would arrest Mum. Chloe felt a fresh wave of anger at Archie.

She could say that George stole the jewels. It would be no more than he deserved. Well, maybe a little bit more. She dismissed the idea.

Or she could return the jewels somehow, which would be difficult now that the police were watching the house. She doubted she'd get past the detective without being spotted.

Then there was the option of telling Mum. It wasn't an appealing thought. Mum would freak out and then hand the stolen treasure in. The police would decide she stole the jewels, and they would lock her up. Chloe imagined her mum cowering in a cell with a large scary woman with a tattooed face and boulders for fists.

The same thoughts kept going round and round in her head, and none of them worked. She couldn't hide the jewels in the house nor leave the

building with them. And nobody would believe her if she told the truth.
The situation was hopeless.

She buried her face in her hands. As she eased her fingers apart, she
noticed a blurred shape—the locket on her bedside table. The brown
hair still lay slightly curled behind the glass. She let out a small gasp. She'd
been wearing it when Archie came alive. Could it be that simple?

She lifted the chain over her head and let the locket rest below her neck.
After a few seconds, a blue mist tunnelled into her skin. It was barely
visible, but Chloe saw it.

'George!' she shouted and jumped off the bed. 'George, I know why
we couldn't see Archie!'

'Leave me alone,' he shouted from his room.

'Fine. I'll do it on my own.' She grabbed a small roll of tape from her
stationery stash, put it in her pocket and charged upstairs into her mum's
bedroom. Her mum's chair was buried under clothes, so she shoved
them onto the bed and dragged the chair out to under the attic. She cast
an irritated look downstairs towards George's bedroom, then climbed
onto the chair and used a hooked stick to open the hatch. It fell open
and slammed back into the ceiling.

Chloe hooked the ladder, jumped off the chair, and gave it a hard pull.
It slid through its runners and hit the floor.

George shouted up the stairs. 'What are you doing?'

'Getting Archie.'

'Don't!'

Chloe scaled the ladder, climbed into the dark enclosure, and pulled
the light cord. The dim bulb just about lit a path through her aunt's
unloved gadgets to Archie. She approached slowly, holding the locket
in her hand for comfort, and then let it fall back against her skin. She
opened Archie's casket and waited.

'It's okay,' she said. 'I won't freeze.'

Archie frowned.

Chloe's mouth fell open. It had really worked. She backed up a little. A knot of fear twisted her stomach.

'You can see me?' Archie asked.

Chloe nodded.

Archie allowed himself a slight smile. 'Wow.'

He pushed the casket door open and clambered out.

Chloe glared at him. 'There's a policeman at the door. I think he knows.'

Archie looked down at the floor. 'I'm sorry. I was lonely.'

'Just help me fix things.'

Archie nodded.

'I need one of your hairs for George; it's how I can see you.' She indicated the locket containing the hair.

Archie looked confused. 'So, all I had to do was give you a hair, and you'd have been able to see me?'

'Yep.'

'It wasn't the jewels?'

'Nope.'

'That's annoying,' Archie said.

'Just a bit. What's also annoying is we're all about to be arrested.'

Archie plucked a hair out. He looked at it. 'Why didn't you see me when you held me?'

Chloe was stumped for a moment. 'Perhaps the magic is in the root? It needs to be pulled out to release its energy. I don't know. I'm not an expert on magical toy bears!'

Archie looked at a bald patch where the robot had taken a handful. 'So, others who have my hair could see me?'

'If they know what to do.' Chloe took the hair. She got the tape out of her pocket, tore off a small section, stuck the hair in the middle, and loosely stuck the tape to her arm. 'Let's go.'

She kept an eye on Archie as she backed towards the opening. This all seemed impossible, and she half expected him to crumple to the floor any second. She studied him as though expecting to find clues, hidden wires, electrical motors—

Her thoughts were so tied up with the mystery of Archie's existence that she reversed into a wooden lip that ran around the hatch. 'Oh!' she yelped as she fell backwards.

Archie lunged forward to grab her hand.

Chloe reached out, and for a second, they almost touched.

Archie hit the floor face down as Chloe fell backwards through the open hatch.

Her mind flashed through everything she hadn't gotten around to doing. All the places she'd never get to visit—

And then she came to an abrupt but painless stop. She looked up into her brother's face.

'You could have died!' he shouted as he buckled but held her in his arms.

Archie appeared at the top of the ladder. Chloe pulled the tape off her arm, stuck it to George's forehead so that the hair was pressing against his skin and pointed up.

George looked up at Archie. He froze, still holding his sister.

Chloe frowned.

The tape took on a blue tint. Chloe waited as the hair did its magic.

Archie climbed down a few steps.

George gradually came round. He looked at Archie, his brow furrowed.

Archie took another step.

George dropped Chloe.

'Owwww!' Chloe cried as she hit the floor.

'What *is* it?' George moaned and backed away. 'Why's it moving—?'

'You don't need to worry,' Archie said.

George screamed.

'Calm down, George,' Chloe urged.

'It sp-sp-speaks!'

Archie took a step towards George.

George backed away further. He looked around for a weapon—something he could wave at the unholy creature walking towards him.

'It's okay, George,' Chloe said. 'You're not going crazy, but Archie is alive. He thought taking the Crown Jewels would prove it.'

'I've been overdoing the computer games. It's done something to my mind.'

'George, we don't have time. Mum will be back shortly, and if we don't calm down, the policeman will know something's up.'

George was numb.

'George, do you want us all to end up in prison?' Chloe shook his arm.

'B-b-but we didn't do anything,' George stuttered. He turned to Archie. 'What are you?'

Archie looked to the sky. 'I wish I knew.'

'Some sort of machine, maybe,' George mumbled.

Archie shrugged. 'Not that I'm aware.'

Chloe glared at Archie, wishing he would keep quiet, then turned to George. 'If it helps, then yes, he's a machine.'

George nodded, glad of any rational explanation. 'Okay, good.'

Archie frowned. 'I don't think I'm a machine.'

Chloe shook her head. 'You're not helping!'

They heard the key downstairs as Edith let Detective Masters into the house.

CHAPTER 25

DETECTIVE MASTERS WIPED HIS feet on the mat inside the porch.

'Come through,' Edith said as she led him to the front room.

Masters took his time and looked around as he followed.

Edith gestured at the sofa. 'Please, take a seat.' She also sat down, hitting the armchair heavily and put out a hand out to steady herself. 'How can I help?'

Masters checked out the front room. 'Nice house.'

'Yes. It's not mine. My sister's abroad. I'm just staying here until I sort my life out... Sorry, you didn't need to know that.'

Masters smiled. He studied the photos on the mantelpiece and was drawn to an aerial photo of the house.

'Is that this house?'

'Yes, I think my son, George, may have taken that one—what's this about, detective? I really should check on my children. They've got a bug or something.'

'I'll be quick. Are you aware the Crown Jewels were stolen recently?'

'Of course. Do you have any leads?'

Masters frowned. She sounded truthful—anxious maybe, but people often were when the police turned up at the door. As he considered how to proceed, he noticed a dark hair on the sofa's arm. He picked it up and looked at it. 'Do you have a dog?'

Edith looked flustered. 'No... maybe my sister had a guest with a pet.'

He held on to the hair, twirling it between his fingers as he studied it. For a moment, he almost thought he saw a bluish light seeping through it and into his hand. He gave his head a tiny shake. Just a trick of the light, he told himself, and he twirled the hair again.

Archie, Chloe and George stood on the landing and strained to listen to the conversation with the detective downstairs.

Chloe moaned. 'I can't hear them. Archie, can you hear them? Do bears have better hearing than humans?'

'Sadly not,' Archie answered.

'He's not a bear,' George said. 'I don't know what he is, but definitely not a bear.'

Chloe huffed. 'Bear or not, he may have better hearing.'

Archie interrupted. 'George, would you mind retrieving the jewels for me? You have a bit of a height advantage.'

'What?' Chloe said. 'Why?'

'I admit, you humans do seem to grow unnecessarily tall—'

'Why do you want them?' Chloe said with a stern tone.

For a moment, Archie seemed baffled by her response. 'The detective could come up any minute. I've got to get them away, and if he sees me, he'll just freeze.'

'Makes sense,' George agreed. Avoiding Archie as much as possible, he nipped down the hallway and into Chloe's bedroom.

Chloe ran after him. 'No, it doesn't! If Archie freezes him, he'll know something happened and never leave us alone.'

'We need them gone,' George said and climbed onto the bed frame.

'You're not thinking this through,' Chloe moaned. 'We need to make a plan!'

'We have no choice.'

Chloe could hear the fear in her brother's voice. There was no reasoning with him. Sometimes it felt like she was the adult in the house, and it was annoying.

Archie searched for something to hold the jewels.

'And anyway, he'd need a search warrant!' Chloe said. 'If he had one, he'd be up here already.'

'Not if Mum allows him to look around. And there's no reason she won't.' He pulled the sceptre from the top of the wardrobe, his hand shaking.

'George, stop! We need to talk about this!'

George grabbed the rest of the jewels and jumped from her bed, causing a loud bang to reverberate through the house.

Chloe looked at him in shock. 'Could you make any more noise!'

Archie spotted a sports bag. 'Mind if I borrow this?'

Chloe ignored him, so he took it as a yes and emptied the bag's contents onto the floor. George manoeuvred around Chloe and passed Archie the jewels, which he secured inside the holdall. He also found a carrier bag and used it to cover the Sceptre, which was too long to fit entirely inside.

Chloe shook her arms in frustration and barred the door. 'No, I won't let you!'

'Chloe!' George said in frustration. 'Get out of the way, please!'

'No, I won't!'

George forced himself into the doorway and created a small space for Archie to squeeze through.

Masters leaned forward from the sofa in Edith's front room. He was still holding Archie's hair between his fingers. 'I'll get to the point of my visit. We found some dark hair at the crime scene. It seems likely they belonged to a rather famous toy bear or puppet that used to be in a children's TV show. Name of Archie. Does that mean anything to you?'

Edith wiped her forearm across her head and shifted uncomfortably. 'Ms Moran?'

'You think a toy bear was involved with the theft of the Crown Jewels?'

Masters smiled. 'I'm sure he wasn't. But please, Ms Moran, answer the question if you wouldn't mind.'

'Edith, please. Yes, I know it. My grandfather worked on the show.'

'Do you have any idea what happened to Archie?'

She tried to appear natural and, in doing so, achieved the opposite. 'No.'

Masters sat back. 'Edith, you don't look like a jewel thief. I'm not accusing you. If you have Archie, I don't care. I'm far more interested in the Crown Jewels.'

Edith squirmed. 'Well—'

BANG

They both looked up towards where George had just jumped from Chloe's bed.

'Perhaps I should check the house for you,' Masters said, getting up.

Edith quickly stood. 'It'll just be George. He's a little heavy-footed.'

'I thought they were ill,' Masters said as he walked into the hallway.

Edith followed and squeezed in front of him. 'Detective, I'm not sure what you hope to find here, but I don't want to worry my—'

Archie came running down the stairs with the sports bag. The Sovereign Sceptre's diamond-encrusted cross peeked through a rip in the bag. Archie saw Masters... and Masters saw him.

Masters gasped, raising his hand. For a second, he doubted his vision--what was he seeing? And was that the Sovereign Sceptre?

Archie's eyes widened.

'Stop!' Masters shouted.

Archie looked terrified, but he didn't stop. He lowered his head and ran for the front door.

'Step aside, Ms Moran,' Masters said as he tried to get past her, but something wasn't right. Edith was as still as a statue. She wasn't breathing, and her mouth was open, frozen mid-sentence. He grabbed her arm in panic, releasing the hair he'd been holding.

Masters caught sight of Archie disappearing through the door, which was the last thing he remembered before he froze.

ele

Chloe looked at George in shock. He was still barring the doorway to her bedroom, and Archie was gone.

'It's for the best,' George said.

'For the best? He's just run off with the Crown Jewels in Mum's sports bag!'

'Mum's?'

'My strap broke.' She dug her fist into her side. 'Do you think Mum will mind if the Crown Jewels are found in her bag?'

'Well, it's not ideal....'

'Oh, and I think there's something from school in the pocket with her name and address on it.'

Chloe pushed George aside and charged down the stairs. She almost ran into the frozen detective in the doorway. 'No... Archie, what have you done...' She ran outside after him.

George followed, giving the detective a terrified glance on his way past.

Chloe charged after Archie. She may be small, but she ran like a racehorse.

'Chloe, leave him,' George shouted, but he was already breathless.

'No,' Chloe screamed and ran faster. 'Hello, Mrs Johnson,' she shouted to an elderly woman who had frozen mid-stride, walking frame suspended in the air.

Archie was tiring, and Chloe quickly caught up and planted herself in front of him. 'Archie, give me the bag.'

'What for?' Archie said.

'Because if you hand in the jewels in Mum's bag, they'll trace it back to her!

'How?'

'Apart from the fact that I'm pretty sure our address is in the pocket, they'll be Mum's and my DNA all over it!'

'Her what?'

She sighed. 'Humans have DNA in their bodies. It's like a unique code. It's found in our cells and can be used to identify people.'

'Oh,' Archie said, although he obviously did not understand.

George caught up; he bent over with his hands on his knees as he recovered. 'She's right, Archie. I didn't even think about that.'

'Also,' Chloe continued, 'If the world learns about you, it would be bad... really bad. For you, I mean. And most importantly, I don't trust you.' She snatched the bag back from Archie.

'You don't trust me?' Archie repeated.

'Why would I, Archie? You stole them in the first place. Who knows what you're capable of?'

Archie stood rigid, numbed by the painful exchange. 'I would never do anything to hurt you further. I just want to help.'

Chloe looked back towards the house. Any second now, the detective would come running up the road. 'George, we've got to go.'

George turned towards home—his bedroom, his games console. 'I don't know. This is big.'

Chloe stared at him with such disappointment that George appeared to shrink. 'We don't have time to discuss it.' She turned to Archie. 'Thanks for ruining our lives.'

She ran, and George reluctantly followed, leaving Archie standing sad and alone on the pavement behind them.

CHAPTER 26

MASTERS AND EDITH EMERGED from their frozen state in her hallway.

Edith blinked rapidly. She looked confused, as did the detective. She called up the stairs. 'George? Chloe? Are you okay?' There was no answer, so she was about to investigate when Masters put a hand on her shoulder.

'Ms Moran, please tell me what's going on.'

'I don't know!' Edith moaned, raising her arms in frustration. 'My grandfather took Archie. He cared about him for some reason, and then he was handed down to me. But everything has been weird since I took him out of his box a few days ago. Sometimes I think—oh, I don't know what I think.' She massaged her head. 'I just need to check on Chloe and George.'

Edith ran upstairs, and Masters made his way to the front door. There was no sight of Archie.

Edith returned. 'They're gone!'

Masters nodded. 'I'll get them back.'

Concern lined Edith's face. 'Where have they gone? I don't understand. I'm going with you.'

'They'll probably return as soon as I leave.' He pulled out a card from his jacket and gave it to her. 'Please, wait here and call me as soon as you see them.'

Edith took the card.

'We'll talk soon,' Masters said and left before she could argue.

Masters crossed the road, climbed into his car, and pulled on his seatbelt. He thought about what had happened. It was like Potters Fields, except before he froze, he'd held what he suspected was one of Archie's hairs. He stroked his face and took out his wallet with the small bag of hairs. They looked unremarkable, but he knew what he'd seen. He retrieved a packet of mints from the glove box, peeled off the small circle of adhesive tape which kept them shut and stuck a couple of hairs to his forearm. A wispy haze of blue light burrowed into the pores of his skin, just as he thought he'd imagined in Edith's living room. He shook his head in wonder. 'Well, I never.'

Masters radioed police headquarters. 'Yeah, hi. It's Detective Eddie Masters, badge number six-zero-nine-two. I believe I've spotted the Crown Jewels. I need the helicopter out immediately. Suspects are a girl of twelve and a boy of fourteen… and they may have a large bear puppet with them. No, this is not a hoax.'

He spent another minute convincing the operator before he ended the call. Time wasted. It occurred to him that Chloe, George, and the bear may have hidden nearby. They might even be watching, waiting for him to leave. He decided to look around on foot.

And then, in the calmness of the car, the strangeness of the situation fully hit him—Archie, a toy from a sixties TV show, was alive.

CHAPTER 27

CHLOE CHARGED ALONG THE road, gripping the bag containing three of the world's most famous treasures hard enough to turn her knuckles white.

'Where are you going?' George shouted as he struggled to keep up with her.

'I don't know... Maybe the Tower of London. We could wipe them down, find a clean carrier bag and leave them next to someone who works there—'

'That's crazy... Will you just *wait!*'

'No!'

'Shouldn't I get a say in this? I am the oldest!'

'So?'

'There are cameras all over the Tower of London. What do you think will happen when they check the footage?'

Chloe skidded to a stop and lowered the bag to the floor. Of course, George was right. She turned to him in defeat. 'I... I don't know what to do.'

George caught up and took a few deep breaths.

Chloe looked down and, with a slight gasp, rearranged the plastic bag covering the sceptre, which was working its way through the carrier.

'Maybe we should have stayed with Archie,' George said. 'He could have helped.'

'Perhaps,' Chloe admitted. 'Or maybe we shouldn't have let him run off with them in the first place!'

George looked a little guilty. 'We could just hand them into the police?'

'We'd have to explain how we have the jewels without mentioning Archie. They'd know we were lying.'

George was about to respond when a car pulled up beside them. The window lowered, and a brawny man leaned out.

'Chloe, George, come here,' the man demanded.

Chloe turned to the car and felt nauseous. It was all over. It was Mr Preston, their PE instructor. She and George exchanged terrified glances.

'I said, come here. Now.'

They approached the car.

Mr Preston looked out of the car window at the sports bag. 'What have you got in there?'

George gulped. 'It's—'

'School project, sir,' Chloe interrupted. 'I had to make a replica of the Crown Jewels.'

Mr Preston looked at his watch. 'You're late.'

'Sorry, sir,' Chloe said. 'We were feeling unwell.'

'At the same time?'

They nodded.

'Likely story. Well, get in.'

Chloe rubbed her stomach. 'We'd like to walk, sir, if that's okay. The fresh air helps.'

Mr Preston glared at Chloe. 'It's not okay. Get in, please.'

They climbed into the back of the car and exchanged nervous glances as they drove to school. 'What are we going to do?' Chloe whispered but stopped talking when she caught Mr Preston looking at her in his rear-view mirror.

The school gate loomed in front of them. Mr Preston drove up and held a pass out to a small window on a metal column. The gates swung open, and he pulled into a reserved space as the gates clanged shut.

The noise rattled Chloe's bones. They might as well be prison gates.

Mr Preston got out of his car and waited for them to follow suit. 'Come on then.'

Chloe looked at the school. It had never appeared more intimidating. She climbed out, followed by George, and they followed Mr Preston along a path and through the main entrance towards Chloe's first lesson. George sneaked a look at the bag.

Mr Preston watched him. 'I don't believe you're in year eight, George? Or has your brief illness made you younger?'

'No sir,' George said.

'Off you go then. I take it you can find your own way?'

'Yes sir,' George muttered and reluctantly left.

Chloe opened the classroom door and walked in front of her class-mates, who sat at rows of desks watching her. Two desks were placed together in the corner to form a display stand.

'You're late, Chloe,' her art teacher, Miss Thomas, said.

'I wasn't feeling well, Miss.'

'Is that your project?'

'Err, yes, Miss.'

'Another early one. Put it with the rest, please and take your seat.'

'Yes, Miss.'

Her teacher continued drawing on the board—a grouping of 3D blocks above and below the horizon line. But Chloe's classmates found her late arrival far more interesting than a load of cubes.

Chloe looked at the collection of replica jewels crafted from all man-ner of household materials. A few of them were good, but even so, the real Crown Jewels would stand out somewhat. She glanced at her teacher. Due to the room's shape, the display was not directly within her view—but that wouldn't save her for long.

Chloe moved things around to make room. She exhaled slowly, drew out the metre-long gold Sovereign Sceptre with the huge Cullinan diamond, and placed it on the display stand.

An awed silence drifted across the class. 'Whoa!' one boy exclaimed, quickly joined by several 'Oohs' and a couple of 'Wows!' One overly excited boy farted, and the class broke into a fit of giggles.

Miss Thomas turned. 'Who passed wind?' The culprit had a bright red face, which gave it away slightly. She glared at him but decided not to embarrass the boy further. 'Just keep it down, please.'

Chloe placed the Imperial State Crown beside the sceptre to further gasps from her classmates.

'I asked you all to keep it down,' Miss Thomas said. 'Chloe, sit down, please.'

'Yes, Miss.' Chloe placed the golden orb with the rest and quickly attempted to cover the jewels with her classmates' efforts.

Miss Thomas looked across the classroom, seeking out the source of the disturbance. 'Okay, who can tell me what the drawing on the board is an example of?'

One girl put her hand up.

'Yes, Sally,'

'It's one-point perspective. Miss, can we look at Chloe's project?'

'We'll look at them all Monday; that was the agreed deadline.'

'But—'

'No buts, all eyes to the board, please. I would like you to—'

A piercing, drill-like bell sounded. Several children jumped, and even more put their hands over their ears.

Miss Thomas put her piece of chalk down. 'Okay, class. Follow me to the exit.'

The class groaned.

'Come on. This could be real. Quickly, please. Fire alarms should not be ignored.'

The children grabbed their coats and followed behind Miss Thomas. Chloe held back. Perhaps this would be her opportunity to remove the jewels.

'Come on, Chloe,' Miss Thomas shouted. 'There's nothing here worth dying for.'

You don't know what's here, Chloe thought. She dragged her heels but left as instructed.

CHAPTER 28

AFTER A THOROUGH SEARCH of the local area, Detective Masters returned to his car. He sat with his hands on the wheel, organising his thoughts until he was distracted by the approaching police helicopter. He watched it circle the area for a moment, then turned the ignition key, pulled away and took a right turn at the end of the road.

'Pull over here, please,' a shaky voice said.

Masters jumped. 'What the—' He looked in the mirror but couldn't see anything. He pulled over to the side of the road and turned as a toy bear climbed up from the floor in the car's rear.

Masters gawped at the strange stowaway.

'You should lock the door when you leave the car,' Archie said. 'There are some dishonest people around.'

Masters blinked. 'What are you?'

'Charming,' Archie said and tried to smile.

The detective looked Archie over, but nothing about him made any sense. 'I don't understand....'

'I get that a lot lately. But I'll get to the point. Yes, I'm alive, and I took the Crown Jewels.'

Masters could see his mouth moving and hear him, but this was impossible. He turned back to the front and stared forward. He caught sight of Archie in the mirror. 'You're alive?'

'Seems that way.'

Masters waited as if he expected Archie to evaporate. After a couple of minutes, though, Archie was still waiting patiently. It was time to accept the facts in front of him. 'Right...' He closed his eyes and opened them again. 'You stole the jewels?'

'I prefer borrow.'

'I think you'll find that to borrow something, you need the owner's permission. Did you ask the King?'

Archie shook his head. The detective continued to stare at him.

'Right.... Maybe we'll come back to that. Can I ask why you did it?'

Archie sighed. 'Chloe had to make a copy of the jewels for home-work—well, some of it. I thought if I got the real ones for her to copy, she'd realise I was alive. It gets lonely when no one can see you.' He noticed the hair stuck to Masters' forearm. 'I didn't know about the hair thing at the time. Normally, anyone that sees me freezes. It's horrible.'

'I can't believe I'm talking to a toy bear,' Masters mumbled as he turned back.

'I'm not a toy.' Archie looked through the window as the Police heli-copter made another pass.

'What's your full name?' Masters asked.

'It's just Archie.'

'I'm sorry, Archie, but I have no choice but to do this. Archie, I arrest you for the theft of the Crown Jewels. You do not have to say anything. But it may harm your defence if you do not mention when questioned something which you later rely on in court. Anything you do say may be given in evidence. Do you understand?'

Archie shook. 'Yes.'

Masters dragged handcuffs out of the glove box.

'Where are the Jewels?' he asked as he passed the handcuffs to the back. 'Put these on, please.'

Archie put his paws into the cuffs, and Masters banged them shut. 'Chloe and George have them. They're hoping to return them, but they'll be caught and get in trouble. It's time for me to put things right.'

'Do you know where they are now?'

'I tried to follow, but someone pulled over and asked them to get in. I think it may have been a teacher.'

'Which school do they go to?'

'I don't know the name, but it's over Tower Bridge towards the Tower of London and then a few minutes' drive.'

Masters nodded. 'I think I know the one. While I drive, could you talk me through what happened on the day of the robbery?'

Archie winced at the word *robbery* but agreed.

Masters flicked a switch, and a police siren sounded. He put his foot down and sped forwards.

The school building emptied, and pupils gathered in groups and chatted while waiting for the fire brigade to arrive and check that the building was safe. Chloe had separated herself from her classmates. She needed space to think.

'Chloe!' a hushed voice called.

She looked around.

George was standing behind a tree. He beckoned Chloe to join him.

Chloe waited until Miss Thomas was looking the other way and ran to the tree. George held the sports bag, which once again contained the Crown Jewels.

Chloe gaped at George. '*You* set off the fire alarm!'

'What choice did I have? Did Miss Thomas see the jewels?'

'I can't believe you did that. And no, she didn't.'

George nodded. 'Good.'

Chloe looked towards the school gates. 'We can't just leave.'

'You were the one that said we had to protect Mum.'

Chloe pushed the fear away. Leaving school without permission was unthinkable to her, but George was right. 'Okay, let's do it. Where are we going, anyway?'

'I get a say now, do I?'

'Maybe.'

'We'll work it out on the way.' George said.

Chloe frowned. 'That's the stupidest thing I've ever heard.'

'Let's head towards home.'

Chloe gave a slight smile. 'And the Tower of London.'

George ignored her.

As Masters and Archie sped around the corner, they heard the unmistakable shriek of a fire alarm.

'I doubt that's a coincidence,' Masters said. He slowed to look at the children grouped by class. 'See them?'

Archie scanned the area and shook his head.

'Keep your eyes open, but don't let anyone see you.'

Difficult advice to follow, Archie thought, but he kept himself low.

'Any thoughts on their destination?' Masters asked.

Archie lifted his head a little. 'My guess would be the Tower of London.'

'I don't have any better ideas,' Masters said. He turned around and drove towards the Tower.

After a few minutes, Archie's head jerked towards something. 'Over there, by the lamppost!'

Masters saw where Archie was pointing and ran his car up on the pavement. 'Stay down,' he ordered Archie. Pedestrians were staring at him as he jumped out. 'Chloe, George. Get in the car!'

Chloe and George looked around for an escape route as passers-by stared at them.

'Archie is with me,' Masters said quietly. 'I told him to stay low.'

Chloe looked doubtful until Archie popped his head up for a second and gave a little wave. She lifted her hand to wave back, but Masters gave her a slight shake of his head, and she let her hand drop back to her side.

Masters gave a reassuring smile to the nearby pedestrians. 'Nothing to see, just a couple of truants.'

Chloe glared at him.

George turned to Chloe. 'Let's get this over with.'

Chloe reluctantly followed George to the car.

George deposited the Crown Jewels on the passenger seat before climbing in the back. Chloe also got in the back. Archie was between them.

'Are those the jewels?' Masters asked as he climbed in.

Chloe and George nodded.

'All three items?'

They nodded again. Masters pulled back the plastic bag until the head of the Sovereign Sceptre emerged. He whistled and pulled away, bumping down the kerb back onto the road.

'Archie,' Chloe said, 'what happened?'

'I handed myself in.'

'How come?'

'Seemed the right thing to do.'

'That was very brave.' She leaned closer. 'And really stupid.'

'I had to,' Archie said.

Masters shook his head. He still couldn't believe this was happening. The mood in the car was sombre.

Finally, the police station came into view.

'What will happen to me?' Archie asked.

Masters shifted uneasily. 'I don't know.'

'I do,' George said. 'He's a sentient toy bear. This is unheard of. Some secret government department will take Archie and pull him apart.'

'George!' Chloe scolded. 'Don't.'

Archie's eyes were large with fright.

Masters glimpsed Archie's face in the mirror. He quickly turned back before pity overwhelmed the need for justice. The car became deathly silent.

'I'm sorry, Archie,' Masters said as the police station loomed, 'but you stole the Crown Jewels. What choice do I have?'

Archie stared at the approaching building. 'I understand.' His voice wavered. 'It's my own fault.'

Masters stared forward, a troubled frown on his face.

They were nearly at the police station. Chloe squeezed Archie's paw to comfort him. Masters should have indicated to turn, but he didn't. He kept on driving. They watched the Police Station recede into the distance.

'I need time to think,' Masters said. 'Unfortunately, what George said may not be far from the truth. You present me with a problem. I don't want to get your hopes up or anything, but are you all okay with going to my place for a bit? It's a little irregular, but under the circumstances—'

'Yes!' they said as one.

Masters gave a half-smile and continued driving. It wasn't long before he turned off the main road. Ten minutes later, Masters pulled up outside his small back garden. He surveyed the neighbourhood. A couple of curtains twitched. 'It's best we don't all go in the front. Neighbourhood watch are quite vigilant here. I'll let you out and meet you at the garden door. You won't run away, will you?'

'You know where we live,' Chloe said.

'And I handed myself in,' Archie added.

Masters nodded. 'Okay, fair enough. I'll keep the jewels with me if you don't mind.'

Archie gazed out of the car window. 'I'll go first. If anyone's watching, they'll freeze.'

'Okay...' Masters said. He still couldn't quite get his head around the fact that the bear was talking to him. Archie climbed over Chloe and got out of the car. They gave Archie a few seconds' head start, then Chloe and George followed, and Masters drove off.

A minute later, Masters opened the back door and ushered them inside. They followed him through a small but tidy kitchen into a hallway and then through a door into an equally tidy lounge-diner.

They passed a sturdy dining room table and onto the front room area. At Masters' request, the children and Archie flopped onto a comfortable three-seater sofa. Masters put the Crown Jewels bag on the floor. The room was sparsely decorated, with a sturdy coffee table, modest-sized television on a small unit, and a piece of modern art on the wall—all coloured interlocking shapes.

Chloe glanced at the art.

Master followed her gaze. 'It was a present,' he explained.

'Nice,' Chloe lied.

'You can have it if you like,' Masters teased, and Chloe's face dropped. He gave her the keys to the handcuffs. 'Perhaps you could do the honours.'

Chloe undid Archie's handcuffs.

Archie shook his paws. 'Thanks.'

Masters flicked on a radio for background noise and then opened the bag to inspect the contents. 'Wow... you certainly know how to make an impression, Archie.'

Masters' large brown cat padded into the dining room.

'Hello, Roswell,' Masters said and leaned down to pet the animal.

Roswell ignored him, scratched himself, and walked up to the couch. He looked from Chloe to George to Archie and stopped. The cat moved its head from side to side and let out a slight hiss.

Archie patted his legs, encouraging the cat to come and say hello. 'Hello, Roswell.'

Roswell considered Archie for a moment longer, moved closer, sniffed his legs, and jumped onto his lap. He dug his claws into Archie's legs, kneaded them, and then settled.

'It seems my cat likes you,' Masters said.

Archie eyed the cat nervously. 'An excellent judge of character.'

Masters paced around. 'What's your mum's number?' he asked.

'Why?' Chloe asked.

'She needs to hear the truth.'

Chloe nervously chewed at her lip. 'What, everything? I'm not sure she's up to it.'

'Oh, I'm sure she's tougher than you think. It's being kept in the dark that upsets people.'

Chloe looked a little offended. 'You don't know her.'

George gave Masters the number. As he dialled, he sunk into the armchair. Edith answered at once.

'Hello.'

'Edith Moran? It's Detective Masters.'

'Have you found them?'

'Yes, they're at my house now.'

'I don't understand... why are they at your house?'

'I find myself in an unusual situation. I can take it down to the station if you'd prefer, but I think there are things you should know first. Archie is here as well.'

'Archie? Why?'

'That's one of the things we should discuss.'

Masters persuaded Edith to leave immediately and gave her his address. He leaned back in his chair. 'I'm sorry, Archie, but I have to ask again; how is this possible? How are *you* possible? Is it A.I?'

Archie looked confused. 'A.I?'

'Artificial Intelligence,' Masters said. 'Is there a super-advanced computer in your head?'

'Not that I know of.'

'It's just that toy bears don't normally come to life. They're not conscious.'

'How are you conscious?' Archie asked.

Masters hesitated. 'I don't know. I don't think anyone really knows.'

'I guess we're not so different, then.'

Masters decided to abandon that line of questioning. 'Let's try another one. Why do people freeze when they see you?'

Archie shrugged. 'Don't know that one either. Jack said I was an abomination to the laws of the universe.'

'Charming,' Masters said.

Archie smiled. 'He was like that, but he was actually very kind. Anyway, he said I shouldn't exist, and that's maybe why humans just shut down. It's your brain's reaction to the impossible.'

Masters pondered this for a moment before turning to Chloe. 'How do you think your mum will react to meeting Archie?'

'Badly,' Chloe said.

CHAPTER 29

THE DOORBELL TO MASTERS' house rang. Chloe jumped. She was dreading telling her mum about the Crown Jewels... and about Archie. She needed to distress, not the other way round.

'Archie, maybe you should nip out for a bit,' Masters said. 'While we prepare Edith.'

'I could jump out and surprise her,' Archie offered. 'You know, make it quick.'

'I don't think so.'

Archie shrugged and tried to move Roswell. The cat regarded him with sad eyes and clung on. 'Sorry, Roswell.' He unhooked the animal and manoeuvred himself out from underneath.

Roswell looked across the sofa at George and hissed. George edged away.

'Oh!' Masters said, seemingly remembering something.

Archie stopped. He plucked a hair out and handed it over. 'I'll be bald at this rate.'

'You might be right,' Masters said, taking the hair. 'I was just going to suggest you stay away from the windows. But thanks anyway.'

Archie's eyebrows joined in mild annoyance, and he traipsed off.

Masters found some tape, ripped off an inch, and attached the hair. He left it on the coffee table, went to the door, and opened it. 'Ms Moran, please come in.'

Edith looked around nervously. 'Call me Edith, please.' She peeked around him down the corridor.

'This must seem quite unusual. Please, come in, and I'll explain.'

She followed Masters to the front room. When she saw Chloe and George, she ran to the couch and hugged them in turn. Roswell jumped off and ran for cover.

'I'm fine, Mum,' George squealed and wriggled to get away.

She ruffled his hair and hugged Chloe again. 'I've been so worried. First, the police turn up—no offence, detective—and then you two run off. And your school phoned. How did you end up at school? What's been going on?'

Chloe's features twisted. 'Err...'

'You may want to brace yourself, Edith,' Masters said.

Edith sat between Chloe and George.

Masters leaned forward and clasped his hands together. 'We'd better start with Archie. He's *unusual*. And priceless. Although we probably shouldn't put a value on him.'

Edith looked confused. 'Priceless? You can get a replica locally for a few hundred. Admittedly, the original Archie would be worth more, but we're still just talking about a puppet with a few metal joints.'

Masters shook his head. 'Did you see the story about sightseers losing time? Some said they saw a toy bear?'

Edith nodded. 'Yes....'

'They saw Archie. Archie is alive.'

She turned slightly and looked out of the corner of her eye at Masters. 'Is this a joke?'

'No, Mum,' George said.

Chloe shook her head.

Masters picked up the tape from the table. 'I need to stick this on your arm.'

Edith laughed uneasily. 'Why?'

'Just do it, Mum,' Chloe said. 'Please.'

Edith frowned but held out her arm. Masters pressed the tape onto her skin, and she looked to Chloe for answers.

'If you don't have one of Archie's hairs, you won't be able to see him. You'll freeze.'

Edith was quiet, but Chloe could see that her mum was making connections.

'Archie, do you want to come in?' Masters called.

Archie emerged from the darkness of the corridor into the dining room. 'Hello, Edith.'

Edith's mouth fell open. She then jumped up and scrambled to the back of the sofa. She looked at the detective. 'What is this? Why's Archie talking?'

'He's alive, Mum,' Chloe said before Masters could answer. She prayed her mum would not start screaming.

Edith slowly shook her head. 'He can't be. He's a puppet....'

Archie now stood at the boundary of the front room. 'I'm sorry for any trouble I caused. I may have made some poor decisions.'

Masters raised his eyebrows.

Edith shivered and looked at her children. 'What does it mean?' She searched their faces for clues.

'Archie stole the Crown Jewels,' Chloe said.

'Borrowed,' Archie mumbled.

Masters let out a small sigh. 'I was going to ease into that...' He fetched the sports bag, placed it on the coffee table and uncovered the jewels. 'These were at your house.'

Edith looked almost as if she'd frozen again. But after a moment, her expression relaxed, and she approached the bag. 'This is a joke, isn't it? They're not the Crown Jewels. And Archie is some sort of intelligent machine.' Before anyone could stop her, she pulled the Sovereign Sceptre from the bag and brought the enormous diamond to her face. 'Oh....'

Masters took the sceptre from her and slid it back into the bag. 'Exactly.'

Edith collapsed back onto the sofa.

'Now you see why I asked you here,' Masters said.

Edith stared blankly but managed a slight nod.

Archie edged a little closer. 'I thought if I got Chloe the real jewels, it would prove I'm alive.'

Edith jolted as Archie spoke. She blinked rapidly. 'This can't be happening.'

'That was my reaction,' Masters said. 'But it seems it is.'

Edith got to her feet. 'Would you mind if I had a moment alone?'

Masters stood. 'Of course. It's a lot to take in. Use the kitchen if you like.'

Edith nodded and rushed from the room.

Whilst she was gone, the room descended into an uncomfortable silence. Archie joined Chloe and George on the sofa.

'Do you think I should check on her?' Masters asked after a minute.

'No,' Chloe said, 'I'd give her a couple more minutes.'

'What are you going to do?' George asked the detective.

Masters leaned back and stared at the ceiling. 'I really don't know.'

Edith walked back in, ashen-faced and shaky. Archie jumped up and gave her the seat back.

'Thanks,' Edith said and watched Archie walk away and climb up onto a chair at the dining room table. She lowered herself onto the sofa as though it was a scalding bath.

'Are you okay? Can I get you a tea or something?' Masters asked.

'Have you got anything stronger?'

'Well—'

Edith attempted to smile. 'Tea will be fine.'

Chloe and George opted for cola.

As Masters left, Chloe turned to her mum, 'It'll be okay, Mum.'

'Don't worry about me,' Edith said unconvincingly and patted her daughter's hand.

Chloe's stomach knotted. 'But I do! If you weren't so stressed, we'd still be at home. I mean, our proper home. And I'd still be able to see my friends.'

Edith flinched and took a moment to sort her thoughts out. 'Chloe, I don't want to moan about your father, but he left us in debt... and things were not improving. We couldn't afford to stay.'

Chloe knew all of this. She'd heard the arguments. But other people had problems, and they didn't move to London. 'It's not fair.' As the words left her mouth, she knew she wasn't being fair either.

'No, it's not, but we're lucky. My sister gave me—gave us—a chance to make things better in an exciting city. Or that was the idea. But yes, maybe I should have talked to you both more...' Edith's voice trailed off as more cogs clicked into place. 'Did you know about the Crown Jewels?'

Chloe looked down. 'Not straight away.'

'Why didn't you tell me?'

'You would have handed them into the police and been arrested. We'd have never seen you again.'

'We could have talked about it,' Edith said. 'You could have trusted me.'

'But you wouldn't have listened!'

'That's not fair, Chloe. I know you're unhappy about the move, but it's my job to do what I feel is right for us all.'

'So, what would you have done if I'd told you?'

'I would have handed them in.'

'See, I knew it!'

'I'm sure the Tower of London has enough cameras to prove I wasn't there,' Edith said.

'But how would you have explained why we had the jewels?' Chloe asked. 'Would you have said a magic toy bear stole them?'

Edith gave her a stern look. 'Probably not. But we'd have worked something out. George, did you know about this?'

'Only since this morning.'

'And you didn't think of calling me?'

'Well, I... No, I'm sorry.'

Chloe was stunned. She had fully expected George to say everything was her idea. She gave him a slight smile.

'And the move?' she asked George. 'Are you really okay with it?'

'It's okay, Mum. And Aunt Carole's got more space and faster broadband.'

Chloe looked at George. His priorities really needed some work.

'Okay. Let's get through this, whatever this is,' Edith said, 'and then we'll all have a proper talk about the future. Okay?'

Chloe nodded. It was a small window of hope.

'But I'm still unhappy that you didn't tell me.'

Chloe and George studied their feet.

Edith got up and peeked in the bag with the jewels. 'So... these are the Crown Jewels? I mean, *the* Crown Jewels?'

'Yes,' Chloe said. 'Well, some of them.'

Edith's face drained, and she fell back onto the sofa.

'They have that effect,' Chloe said.

Masters returned with the drinks and put them down. Chloe suspected he'd held back in the kitchen whilst they talked. He disappeared again and, seconds later, returned with a tin of biscuits. 'Help yourselves.'

No one did, although George looked tempted.

Masters noticed Edith looked queasy and covered the jewels back up.

'So, what are we going to do?' Chloe asked.

'I think that's up to the detective,' Edith said.

'Call me Eddie, please. At least in my home.'

'Ed.... I can't. Detective Masters, what are you going to do?'

'If I hand Archie in, I doubt he'll end up in prison. He'll be an oddity, a scientific marvel, something to figure out. And I fear the worst.'

Edith nodded.

A marvel?' Archie repeated.

'And if I don't hand him in, I'll be helping to cover up one of the biggest crimes in history. I could lose my job, reputation, and probably my freedom.'

'Or,' Archie said, 'if you helped return the jewels, you'd be a hero. People would name their children after you. There'd be a statue erected in your honour.'

Masters turned to Archie, 'You're a very optimistic bear.'

'What if,' Edith said, 'and excuse me if I'm out of line here... but what if Archie handed them into the nearest police station?' She glanced at the hair attached to her arm. 'From what I understand from this weird dream I seem to be stuck in, anyone inside would freeze for the duration of his visit, wouldn't they?'

'Some people remember seeing a bear. I mean, seeing Archie. He'd be directly linked to the Crown Jewels.'

'Isn't he already?'

'Well, the soldiers seem reluctant to talk about Archie—that's if they saw him, and I suspect they did. But that may change if further sightings are reported.'

'You make me sound like a UFO,' Archie said.

Masters shrugged. 'It's not far off.'

'Archie could just take them back to where they came from,' George suggested.

'Jewel House is all locked up,' Masters replied. 'At least until they've reviewed their security arrangements.' He got up and paced around his front room. 'And there's the link between Archie and your family. It's best he's not seen, however briefly. After all, it didn't take me long to make the connection.'

Edith let out a long sigh and massaged her temples. The room went quiet.

Chloe's eyes brightened. 'Couldn't you say you found them somewhere?'

'It crossed my mind,' Masters admitted, 'but it's extremely suspicious. It's likely my movements would lead back to you.'

Chloe frowned. 'So, we need to return the jewels—preferably to the Tower of London—without being seen or caught on CCTV.'

They exchanged blank looks, and then Archie perked up. 'How much do the jewels weigh?'

'Hold on,' Masters said, intrigued by the question. He whisked the bag off to the bathroom and returned shortly after. 'Not including the bag, a little over three and a half kilos.'

'Thanks,' Archie said.

'What have you got?' Masters asked.

Archie shifted uncomfortably. 'If I tell you and you decide to trust us, you'd have to lie to everyone, your colleagues, the public—'

The radio in the background caught the group's attention:

'Police have announced a press conference at the Tower of London tomorrow at 3 pm. Our sources state they are ready to divulge everything they know in the hope that the public can assist...'

'I think we should return them before the press conference,' Chloe said, 'or it will just get worse.'

'Archie,' Masters said, 'why don't you share your idea with someone else? Just for now.'

Archie turned to Edith. 'Edith, would you mind hearing me out?'

Chloe and George looked at her expectantly.

'Oh... err, well, okay. Let's go then.'

When Edith and Archie returned, Edith seemed cautiously encouraged. Masters, however, looked unhappy.

'Are you okay, detective?' Edith asked.

'I've been thinking about what Archie said, and—assuming I decide I'm able to help—the secrecy isn't going to work. Sorry, but I'm responsible for ensuring the jewels are safely returned.'

'I understand,' Edith said.

Masters' mobile beeped. He looked at it and buried his face in his hands. 'People are wondering where I am. I'm going to have to go. Will you wait for me?'

'Here?' Edith asked.

'There are probably police watching your place, so yes. But you'll wait, yes?'

'Where else would we go?' Edith said. 'Did you know there's a helicopter circling above our street?'

Masters rolled his eyes. 'I'd forgotten about that. I'll have to say it was a false alarm. Although I'm not sure how I'll explain it.'

Chloe smiled. 'I know. Say you saw some fake jewels!'

Masters looked blank.

'I had to make a replica of a few items from the Crown Jewels for art homework. You could say you mistook them for the real ones!'

'Are they made of gold?' Masters asked.

'Gold wrapping paper,' Chloe said, 'with silver stars, but they're tiny. You can hardly see them.'

Masters massaged his head. 'They would need to be very convincing for anyone to believe I mistook them for the real thing.'

'Well, there's only so much you can do with wrapping paper and cardboard.'

'I can't believe I'm even considering this,' Masters said.

'We could improve them,' Edith suggested.

Chloe pulled a glum face. 'I did my best.'

'I've got to go,' Masters announced. He glanced at the bag containing the Crown Jewels.

'Don't worry,' Chloe said, 'we just want to return them.'

George nodded in agreement.

'And you know where we live,' Edith added.

'Don't forget, I handed myself in,' Archie said.

Masters nodded and left.

As Masters drove off, Chloe looked at her mum. 'Do you think he's going to turn us in?'

'No, I'm sure he's not.'

Chloe didn't think her mum looked sure at all.

CHAPTER 30

DETECTIVE MASTERS PULLED IN at the police station and practised smiling in the car mirror. He looked like he had stomach issues, so he quickly gave that up. His job required him to tell the truth, hand Archie in, and return the jewels. And hopefully, Archie would be okay. But he knew he wouldn't be okay. Some secret government department would be desperate to find out what made Archie tick, even if it meant destroying him. The only way to save Archie was to lie, and Masters wasn't happy about it. With a shake of his head, he climbed out of the car and trudged towards the entrance.

As he walked through the office, fellow officers glanced at him, quietly nodded hello and busied themselves with any task they could find. Masters smiled back, gave the occasional nod and continued to the Chief Inspector's door. He steadied himself and gave two knocks.

'In!' his boss shouted.

Masters entered and closed the door behind him.

The Chief Inspector looked at him with beady eyes set into a rosy face. 'Sit down, Eddie,' he said, jowls wobbling.

Masters took a seat in front of a grand desk.

'You used police resources, including a helicopter, to chase two children and a toy bear. Correct?'

Masters looked down for a moment. 'Yes, sir.'

'Would you care to explain why?'

Masters paused as he considered his options, but he had nothing better than Chloe's idea.

'I thought they had the Crown Jewels.'

His boss waited.

'My only lead was the hairs found at the scene, which I traced to a toy manufacturer called Tiny Toys. They made the bear used in The Amazing Archie TV show. They confirmed the hairs matched the original Archie.'

'How could they be sure?'

'The hairs were dyed darker than usual for TV.'

'I'm not sure how relevant a toy bear is to all of this but continue.'

'It's a puppet sir. Anyway, I thought that if I found Archie, I'd find the thieves. The popular theory is that Jack Goodman took him. He worked on the show but died in the early sixties. Jack has two grandchildren living in London who may have received Archie. One is working abroad, so that left Edith Moran. When I went to their house, I saw her children with what I thought were the Crown Jewels.'

'Thought?'

Masters swallowed. 'It turns out the young girl made a replica of the jewels for a school project. I'm not sure what happened, but I lost them. The children ran off—'

The chief inspector crossed his arms and narrowed his eyes. 'So, we had a police helicopter out chasing a girl with a cardboard crown, is that about right?'

Masters nodded. 'It was wrapped in gold paper, sir.'

The Chief Inspector snorted. 'It's not funny, Masters.'

'No, sir, it's not.'

'This girl must be some artist.'

'It was only a glimpse. I made a mistake.'

'If this gets out, the department will be a laughing stock.'

'I'm sorry, sir. If I could get back to work, I'm sure I can sort it out.'

'I'd appreciate it if you would conduct your enquiries at your desk for now. Your outlandish theories are less likely to cause a problem that way.'

'Yes, sir,' Masters said as he rose.

'One more thing. We've decided to hold a press conference at the Tower of London.'

'I heard.'

'I want you to share everything you know. Maybe the public can help.'

'Me, sir?'

'Yes, Eddie. You can talk, can't you?'

'Public speaking is not really my thing, sir.'

'Tough. Write your briefing. I want to read it at eight-thirty tomorrow morning. And leave out today's disastrous events unless you're specifically asked. Just the facts Masters, no speculation.'

'Yes, sir.'

Masters returned to his desk and let out a long sigh. His head sunk for a moment. Then he picked up his phone and dialled a number.

CHAPTER 31

CHLOE SAT SCRIBBLING IDEAS on a pad at Masters' dining room table. The phone rang, causing her pen to slide across the paper.

'I'll get it,' Archie said and jumped off the couch.

'Nooo!' Chloe and George shouted in unison.

Edith just shook her head in disbelief.

'Joke!' Archie said.

The answering machine kicked in. 'Hi, Mum, it's Eddie. I meant to get away for an hour, but something's come up. I have to prepare for a press conference tomorrow afternoon. Anyway, just relax and don't do anything crazy without me.' Masters gave a fake laugh. 'I'll see you soon. Bye.'

'I think that message was meant for us,' Chloe said.

'You reckon?' George said sarcastically.

'Do you think he'll still help us?' Chloe asked. 'He'll have to stand in front of the press and lie. To *everyone*.'

Edith slowly shook her head and then covered her face with a hand.

Archie looked at the floor. Gradually, he lifted his head. 'I did have one idea. I saw a... a *thing* while I was in the attic. Like a little helicopter. We can use it to fly the jewels into The Tower of London.'

Edith looked through her fingers. 'He means a drone. Your aunt bought it to take aerial photos. Another short-lived hobby.'

'That's brilliant!' Chloe said.

George shifted nervously. 'Do you mean, *leave the house?* Detective Masters only said he'd been delayed. He didn't say he wouldn't help!'

'And what if he changes his mind?' Chloe asked. 'Things have changed.'

George shook his head. 'You're mad. He knows about us. What's the point of running?'

'We're not running,' Chloe said. 'We'll just return the jewels without involving him.'

'I'm not sure he'd tell anyone about me anyway,' Archie offered. 'Who'd believe him?'

Edith removed her hands from her face. 'We could leave a note. Ask him to give us until the press conference to get everything sorted out.'

George paced in circles. 'But if we go back to the house, there'll be police there.'

'If he called the helicopter off, the police would also be gone.' Chloe said. 'Well, hopefully.'

Archie held a paw up. 'If there *is* someone there, I can probably help. Also, I may have left the window unlocked in the spare room if that helps.'

'May?' Edith said.

'As in, I know I did,' Archie clarified.

'Right.' Edith looked around the room. 'Hands up if you think we should do it.'

Archie raised his arm.

Chloe followed suit.

'Nope,' George said.

Edith raised her arm. 'Sorry, George, it looks like you're outvoted, and I really think it would be unfair to involve the detective. I'll write a note for him.'

'Is that a good idea?'

'He deserves that much.'

'Why?'

'Because he trusted me. He phoned immediately and told me what was happening. Something neither of you did. Plus, he'd report us to his bosses if we didn't at least leave a note. He'd have no choice.'

George gave up arguing and took solace in the biscuit tin. He grabbed three and scoffed the first one.

'We really thought you'd hand the jewels in and be arrested,' Chloe explained.

'*You* did,' George said to Chloe between mouthfuls.

Chloe tried to disintegrate George with her eyes, but despite her best effort, she couldn't generate deadly laser beams.

George ate another biscuit. 'Fine, leave a note, but please don't put our names on it.'

'Okay,' Edith said, laying out notepaper on the dining room table. She wrote:

We can't involve you any further. Please give us until the press conference to sort this out. Thank you for everything, E. x

Edith folded the note in half and left it on the table.

'Shall we go, E?' Chloe asked.

'It's Mum to you. Yes, let's go.' Edith checked her mobile. 'George, maybe you should turn yours off as well. We don't want anyone tracking us.'

'Already off,' George said and went to eat another biscuit.

Edith looked at him. 'Do you need another biscuit? We'll get something proper soon.'

George rolled his eyes and tossed down the biscuit next to the note. Chloe grabbed the Crown Jewels, and after a quick check that they had everything, they left via the back door.

As Master's back door shut, Roswell emerged from his hiding place. The front room had exciting new smells, so he sniffed around and then jumped onto the coffee table. He pawed at the biscuit tin, but it remained stubbornly shut.

Roswell stretched and looked around the room. His nose twitched, and he climbed onto the back of the armchair. There was something interesting on the dining room table. He wiggled his rear end, then leapt onto the shiny wooden surface and skidded to a halt. Edith's note flew off the table and floated in a zigzag fashion to the floor.

It landed hidden behind the armchair.

Roswell ate George's discarded biscuit.

CHAPTER 32

As THEY NEARED THEIR street, Chloe was the first to spot a police vehicle parked about ten houses up from their own. She silently pointed at the car.

Edith exhaled slowly as she pulled over. She checked the sky for helicopters and found it was clear. 'Could be worse, I guess.'

'How?' George said.

Chloe looked at the side passage. 'We might be okay if we use the side window. I should go. I'm smallest—he's less likely to see me.'

'Technically, I'm the smallest,' Archie said.

Edith stared at the police car. 'He's facing this way. He'll see us.'

'That settles it then,' Archie said. 'I'll sneak up to the car and tap on his window. While he's frozen, I'll get in the car and stay there until you're done.'

'But he'll see you!' Chloe said.

'Only for a millisecond, and he won't understand. Some people remember nothing.'

Edith continued staring forward with fear etched across her face. 'I don't know.'

Archie reached for the door handle. 'I do. It's the only way. I'll signal you.' With that, he climbed out and slunk towards the police vehicle, keeping himself hidden behind parked cars.

A minute later, the police car's wipers started, then stopped. Then a spurt of water shot over the windscreen, and finally, the headlights flashed once.

Edith jumped out and scampered down the side entrance of their house.

'I guess Mum's doing it,' George said.

Chloe watched her mum. 'Hmm.'

Five minutes later, Edith emerged with a large box in a bin bag and a couple of other bags. The car boot wasn't large enough for it all, so Chloe and George budged up, and she placed the box on the back seat, then climbed in and started the engine.

Archie came running towards them and climbed into the front passenger seat. 'You've got a minute and a half before he comes round.'

Chloe grinned at Archie. 'Did you struggle to find the headlight flasher?'

'Maybe,' Archie said quietly.

Edith put the car into drive.

As they passed the police car, they looked inside. The policeman looked young and had slicked-back blond hair. He was now a statue with his head craned towards the passenger side window.

'I hope his neck doesn't ache—all twisted like that,' Edith said.

'I expect he'll survive,' George said.

They drove through London and parked as soon as they found a quiet spot. Chloe was already peering into the bag containing the box.

'Will it work?' Archie asked.

Edith nodded. 'I think so. It's big enough to cope with the weight. My sister certainly doesn't believe in doing things on a small scale.'

Chloe peeled back the bin bag to reveal the contents. The label on the box read *Earth Surveillance X-II Heavy Lift Drone.* 'Cool.'

'Your aunt Carole gave George and me a flying lesson last summer,' Edith said.

'Where was I?'

'Doing something with your dad.'

'Oh, okay.'

Edith gave a slight smile. 'The ES-twelve,' she said in a knowledgeable voice, impersonating her sister, 'has more lift for your pound than any other drone.' She returned to her own voice. 'Of course, Carole wanted to attach the best camera, so she needed a large drone. It has a release mechanism. We can land them and fly away.' She skimmed a shaky hand through the air to demonstrate.

'What's in the boot?' Chloe asked.

'Just stuff that might come in handy,' Edith said. 'And the fake jewels you made. I thought we could spruce them up if we get craft supplies. We might need them as an alibi for Detective Masters.'

'They're almost identical to the real thing already.'

'Right,' George said sarcastically.

'I was joking,' Chloe said. 'Obviously.'

CHAPTER 33

DETECTIVE MASTERS ESCAPED FROM work for lunch and raced home, eager to finish his conversation with Archie and friends. He stopped abruptly outside his house, jumped out of his car, and rushed to his front door.

As soon as he entered his hallway, he knew something was wrong. It was too quiet. 'Edith!' he shouted as he went to the front room. His voice echoed around the house. They were gone, and so were the Crown Jewels.

'Chloe! George!' He dashed to the kitchen, colliding with the dining room table on the way. The pain barely registered, and he backtracked and ran upstairs, checking every room.

'Archie!'

Nothing. Masters' stomach turned. With a shaky hand, he pulled out his mobile and called Edith, but her phone was off. Looking to the heavens, he exhaled noisily. 'Where are you all...?'

Masters rushed around the house a second time, even though he knew it was pointless. He then grabbed his jacket and returned to the car where he sat, drumming his fingers on the wheel. *Where would they be?*

He slipped the gear into first and raced away.

CHAPTER 34

EDITH DROVE WITH NO specific destination in mind. George was sitting next to her. Chloe and Archie were in the back.

Chloe was thinking about the last few days' events—it was like she couldn't wake up from a bizarre dream. She glanced at Archie. He was still there and very much alive.

George broke her train of thought. 'I'm not sure the drone is a good idea.'

Chloe sighed. 'What a surprise.'

'It'll be noisy. Everyone will see us. And even if they don't, the police or someone will capture it and find a serial number. That will lead to the shop where Aunt Carole bought it. The shop owner will have Carole's address—and that'll be it. Prison food for the next twenty-five years.'

Chloe shook her head. 'You're so negative!' But he had a point. 'We just need to launch it somewhere noisy or out of the way.'

Archie peered at the endless traffic. 'Noisy shouldn't be hard.' He turned back to the front and noticed a towering hotel in the distance. It was constructed of black stone with sturdy square balconies stretching to the sky. 'What about there?' He pointed at the hotel.

Edith glanced at Archie in the rear-view mirror to see where he was looking. 'The Kraken Hotel?'

'Kraken?' Archie asked.

'It's a giant sea monster,' George said.

'The hotel has a monster theme,' Edith explained with a hint of curiosity.

Chloe snorted dismissively. 'It doesn't matter what it is, Archie. We have no money. We're more economy B&B.'

Edith looked thoughtful. 'That's not entirely true. My sister put some funds on a card in case of emergencies or if the house flooded or something. I don't like to use it.'

'I think this counts as an emergency, Mum,' George said. 'How much?'

Edith was staring at the approaching hotel.

'Mum?'

'Oh, err... three thousand.'

Chloe's mouth fell open. 'Let's stay at the Ritz!'

'If we stay anywhere, we need to be near the Tower of London, not miles away.' Edith looked again at the Kraken Hotel. 'It would be nice to see it....'

'Could we stop at a shopping centre?' Archie asked. 'I think there's a way to prevent anyone from getting hold of the drone.'

'How?' Chloe asked.

'Don't fly it too close,' Archie replied, somewhat mysteriously.

Edith looked scared. 'I don't want to know. Just tell me what you need.'

'Light nylon material, about four meters squared, should do. Or the widest you can find. Strong twine, a few tools—you may have to give me a few minutes to think this through.'

Edith grabbed a notepad and pen from the glove box and passed them back to Archie. 'Write a list. Can you write?'

'Of course,' Archie said.

'Oh yes,' Edith said, 'the note.' She turned to George. 'I'm sorry I didn't believe you.'

'I understand,' George said and smiled to himself. 'And you know what they say. Nothing says sorry like a new Xbox game.'

Edith glanced back at George. 'Subtle.'

A few minutes later, they passed a sign that read 'The Landing—Shopping Heaven.' An arrow showed a right turning two hundred meters ahead.

'Write quickly, Archie,' Edith said. 'I haven't been there, but Carole said they have everything.'

CHAPTER 35

MASTERS STOOD AT EDITH's door and rang the bell. There was no answer, so he peered through the window. The nets obscured his view, but it looked empty. He made his way to the side of the house and tried the spare room window. It edged up an inch. Masters checked no one was watching, slid the window open, and climbed in.

The house was silent. 'Edith? Chloe? George?' he shouted as he stuck his head in each room.

'Archie?' he called, climbing the stairs. But he already doubted himself. Did he really meet a talking toy bear?

Masters retreated to the front room. He spotted a photo of Edith, Chloe and George on the mantelpiece, so he slipped it out of the frame and into his jacket pocket. It might come in useful later.

After a last look, he left the property the way he came in. He returned to his car, sat and stared at the house for a minute, then sighed and set off home.

Back home, Masters went to his office and stared at his laptop as if the answers were hidden inside. He tried Edith's phone again, but there was still no ringtone.

Roswell padded into the office and looked at his owner.

'Where are they, Roswell?'

The cat stared at him.

'What do you think; should I report them now? Or do you think they'll do the decent thing and return the jewels?'

Roswell tipped his head to one side. Once he'd established food was not on offer, he left.

'I should report myself,' Masters mumbled. He switched on a brass desk lamp, pulled a printout of his press release from his jacket pocket, laid it on the desk and started to read. 'Good morning. Thank you all for coming. My name is Detective Eddie Masters. On behalf of The Metropolitan Police, I'm authorised to share what we know about the theft of the Crown Jewels—'

Masters stopped abruptly. He screwed the paper up and hurled it at a bin. Then dug into his pocket and pulled out the photo of Edith, Chloe and George. It was hard to believe the family he'd met—who seemed decent—were on the run.

He slammed the photo down. After a few minutes of sitting in a daze, he got up and went to the kitchen, where he topped up Roswell's bowls with biscuits and water.

Roswell looked at the food with disgust, then at Masters, and then walked away.

'I'll get you some posh pouches on my way home. Fussy animal!'

As he left, he grabbed the photo of Edith and her children.

CHAPTER 36

CHLOE LOOKED OUT OF the window as Edith followed the directions to the car park. The barrier opened, and they drove in circles up to the quiet top level and pulled into a secluded space

'How's that list going, Archie?' Edith asked. H

'One question. Would you mind me making some minor alterations to your back window?'

Edith shrugged. 'Do what you like. This car's days are numbered.' She patted the dashboard comfortingly.

Chloe thought the car's days were *long past* would be a better description.

Archie added a few more lines and passed the list, which Edith gingerly accepted.

Shopping list
Wellington boots – bear sized.
Blocks of wood, 8cmx8cmx20cm, hacksaw. (Try a craft shop)
Short screws/washers
Lightweight nylon material, 4 metres square or larger
Strong, thin twine
Eyelets (to attach twine to the material)
Sewing kit
Strong tape, masking tape, markers, scissors

Gold spray paint for jewels (and anything else that looks good!)
Dark film for car windows
Utility knife
Some sort of screw-in hook (net curtain eyes/hooks should do)
Disguise for the package to draw attention away from the drone—the dafter, the better!
Disposable gloves
Anything else you think would be useful!

'Dark film for car windows?' Edith said, 'Wellington boots?'

Archie looked shifty. 'Perhaps it would be better if I explained later.'

Edith ground her teeth as her resolve crumbled.

'We can do this, Mum, Chloe said.

'But *should* we?' Edith asked.

'It'll be okay,' Chloe said. 'We left the detective a note. We just need to see it through.'

'I'm still prepared to hand myself in,' Archie said.

Chloe shook her head. 'You can't, Archie. Something awful would happen to you. And even *you* don't deserve that.'

'Thanks, I think. Can I make one request?'

Chloe felt Archie was not in a position to make requests, and judging by the silence, she wasn't alone.

Archie continued. 'If anything goes wrong—if we're caught. Tell them the truth.'

'Okay,' George said a little too eagerly.

Edith looked at Archie in the car mirror. 'I'm not sure they'd believe us.'

Archie gave a sad but determined expression. 'I'll make them.'

Edith folded the list up and put it in her pocket. 'Right, we better make sure nothing goes wrong then. You will stay hidden, won't you, Archie?'

'Of course.'

'Be good,' Chloe said to Archie as she climbed out.

'And don't steal anything,' George added.

'I don't know. One small indiscretion....'

As they headed for the lift, Archie stretched out on the back seat. But he soon discovered a curious thing—time passes very slowly in the back of a stationary car. Or at least that's how it felt. After checking the dashboard LED clock for the hundredth time, he popped his head up for a peek. They'd been over an hour already.

The driver parked diagonally opposite was staring directly at Archie. He was now frozen.

'Oops,' Archie said, dropped down and hoped the man would recover and simply drive away.

A couple of minutes passed, and then the door opened beside him. Archie nervously turned....

Chloe smiled at Archie, and he sighed with relief. 'Don't talk to me. I think someone's watching.'

The family noted the warning and ignored Archie as they filled the back seats and car boot with shopping. A nearby car started its engine and drove away.

'Was that a blue car?' Archie asked.

'I believe so,' Edith said as she looked towards the exit.

'I only put my head up for one second, and he was staring straight in.'

'Archie,' George moaned.

'He'll probably think he imagined it,' Chloe said. 'I did.'

Edith looked around. 'Let's get out of here.'

'Where to?' Archie asked.

Edith almost smiled. 'The Kraken Hotel. I've booked us a room.'

'I hope it's got a balcony,' Archie said.

'We're on the fortieth floor.'

Chloe couldn't help but notice that her mum sounded a little excited by the prospect of staying at the Kraken Hotel. She was glad.

Five minutes later, they were almost there. Chloe glanced at Archie. She wondered what it was like to find yourself alive in a strange body. Or maybe it wasn't strange for him. And was he really alive, or was he something else? Archie caught her looking at him. 'Are you okay?' she asked.

'I'm alive, and I have company. What more could I want?'

George glanced at the Crown Jewels. 'Not being chased by the police would be an improvement.'

Chloe pressed on, keen to learn more about her strange companion. 'Did Mum's grandfather ever see you?'

'Jack... Yes, he did, as it happens. I don't know how; we didn't know about the hair thing. He was one of the animators, so he spent a lot of time with me.'

'Maybe he accidentally ate one of your hairs.'

'Do you think that would work?'

Chloe thought for a moment. 'Probably not. I expect a hair would dissolve in stomach acid.'

'You have acid inside you?' Archie asked, wide-eyed.

'Yep.'

'And you think *I'm* strange!'

'You are strange. But I guess Jack must have got one of your hairs on him... somewhere.'

'Anyway,' Archie said, 'he was a good friend. I miss him.'

Chloe gave Archie a sad smile.

'And he told no one about you?' Edith asked.

'Not a soul.'

Edith's mouth flattened. 'He should have told someone in the family.'

'I'm sure he would have done. He just didn't get the chance.'

'I'm sorry, Archie,' Edith said. 'It must have been a difficult time.'

'It was. I still feel kind of bad about it.'

'Why do you feel bad?'

Archie propped himself up a bit. 'I think Jack's colleagues knew that he'd taken me, which made things difficult. Jack thought the show would replace me, but the money people decided the show was too expensive. And so that was it. Jack and his former friends were out of a job.'

'It wasn't your fault,' Edith said.

'And you've got friends now,' Chloe said. 'He'd be happy for you.'

'Friends?'

'Not me, of course,' Chloe joked. 'I'm still angry with you.'

Archie smiled.

'We're here,' Edith said.

'Thank you, Edith.'

'No, I mean, we're *here*.' She pointed out of the window.

They peered through the windscreen. The hotel scratched at the sky, a vast column of black stone and black windows, all with square balconies at the front. Black flags with gold trim and a Kraken emblem were positioned on either side of a grand entrance staircase.

'Wow,' Chloe whispered. 'It's so...' She searched for the right word.

'Imposing,' Edith said.

'Yes! Imposing. I love it.'

Edith followed a sign for the basement car park and drove through an automated gate. They found a relatively quiet corner and parked up.

Chloe delved into one of the bags and pulled out a new white blouse Edith had bought for her. She passed George a sleek black shirt, and Edith had chosen a smart charcoal blazer.

Archie watched a little enviously.

'Here,' Chloe said, passing Archie a package. 'We got you something too.'

Archie grabbed the package. It was a white shirt with faint grey lines. 'For me? I don't know what to say.'

'It's only a shirt,' Edith said. 'It will probably need altering, but if you wait until we get into the hotel, I'll give it a go when we get a quiet moment.'

Archie hugged the shirt to his chest. 'Thank you.'

'Pass the curtain pole,' Edith said.

Archie looked confused.

Edith took the long box Chloe had just slid to the front. 'We just needed the box,' she explained to Archie. She opened it up, discarded the curtain rod, and then gently removed the Sovereign Sceptre from the holdall. 'I can't believe I'm holding this.' She admired the huge diamond set in the heart-shaped clasp at one end. 'Can you imagine digging this out of the ground?'

Chloe nodded. 'Probably feels a bit like finding it in your bedroom.'

Edith trembled. 'Pass me the bubble wrap, please.' She indicated one of the bags, and Chloe pulled out a sheet and handed it over.

George cleared his throat. 'Shouldn't you be wearing gloves to handle that thing?'

'I bought some alcohol wipes,' Edith said. 'We've all touched the jewels, so we'll have to wipe them down in the hotel. And then we'll wear gloves.' Edith wrapped both ends of the sceptre, being careful only to touch the staff, and then slid it into the long box. She exhaled with relief and then wrapped the rest of the jewels.

Chloe jumped out, dragged a new suitcase from the boot, and put it down behind the car. 'You sure about this, Archie? You could turn yourself off or whatever you do, and I'll just carry you in.'

'It's probably better no one sees me,' Archie said. 'It's only for a few minutes.'

Archie checked the coast was clear, hopped down from the car, and got into the case.

Chloe looked down at his curled form, and Archie gave a nod. She shut the lid and was about to pick him up when her mum took him.

'That suitcase is almost as big as you!' Edith said.

Chloe stood a little taller, but she relented and grabbed some bags. George took the drone.

They left the car park and walked along the high street to the front of the hotel. As they approached the grand entrance, a man in a short burgundy jacket with decorative trim and gold buttons, black trousers with a gold stripe, and a round cap ran out to meet them.

'Please allow me, madam,' he almost begged. The bellhop took the suitcase. He grunted. 'Heavy! What's in it, the Crown Jewels?' He laughed at his joke.

Edith was silent. And then, 'Haha, good one.'

Chloe laughed as well. And then George. It was very fake.

The bellhop shrugged and walked with them through to the lobby. The impressive décor distracted Edith. Sketches of monsters from literature, film, myth, and legend hung along the walls. Edith stopped at a drawing of Frankenstein's monster. Frankenstein's author, Mary Shelley, had signed it in the bottom right-hand corner. 'Is that real?' Edith asked.

'Of course,' the bellhop answered. 'Many authors made sketches of their creations. Whilst not always known for their artistic talent, they are fascinating, yes?'

'They are,' Edith agreed.

The bellhop smiled. 'The owners invested a great deal of money acquiring original sketches and paintings to decorate this magnificent hotel.'

Edith looked up at the ceiling. A black monster with sprawling tenta-cles supported eight separate chandeliers. 'Wow!'

'Mum,' Chloe urged as she glanced at the suitcase that contained Archie.

'Yes, sorry. Let's get checked in.'

'The children are impatient to explore, I see,' the bellhop said.

'Probably hungry. You know what kids are like.'

'We have an excellent selection of food here. I can recommend the squid tentacles in ink.'

Chloe smiled. 'Great.'

The reception desk curved out from the wall. Behind it was a stone relief of various sea-dwelling monsters, most with rows of deadly-looking teeth. Edith took out her phone to find the reservation number, keeping it slightly hidden as the device didn't fit in with their current upmarket surroundings. The receptionist took the details

With the bellhop's help, they continued to a spacious lift. There was an eerie painting of Dracula on the back wall in a grand frame.

As Chloe examined it, Dracula's hooded eyes rotated towards her, and he smiled, revealing two long fangs.

Chloe let out a small shriek.

The bellhop laughed. 'Sorry, it looks like a painting, but it's actually a screen set into a frame. Would you like a picture with him?'

'No thanks,' Chloe said as she backed away.

The bellhop smiled politely. 'Each of the main lifts has its own host. The werewolf is my favourite.'

'This is some place,' Edith said.

'It certainly is,' the bellhop agreed. 'If this hotel had to battle another hotel, it would emerge victorious after one humiliating round.'

'You're probably right.'

The lift arrived at the fortieth floor with a ping, and the doors opened.

The bellhop opened the door to their room and gave them a key card. 'Please be careful on the balcony.' He put on a spooky voice, grinning impishly at Chloe. 'If you fell to the ground, your bones would literally explode on impact.'

Chloe gave him a slight smile.

'We'll keep that in mind, thanks,' Edith said.

The bellhop loitered awkwardly.

'Oh, sorry,' Edith said and fished a five-pound note from her purse. She thought about it for a moment and then changed it to a twenty-pound note.

'That's extremely generous, madam. If you need anything at all, please phone reception and ask for Hasani. Enjoy your stay.' He left, gratefully sliding the note into his pocket.

Chloe looked at her mum in shock. 'Twenty pounds!'

'Thought it would be good to have the staff on our side.'

'Oh, okay. Good thinking.'

Edith opened the suitcase.

Archie emerged and coughed. 'That guy was great. I nearly laughed.'

'I'm glad you didn't,' Edith said.

Chloe ran to check out the room. It was huge and as impressive as the exterior. In the centre of the dining area, three black sofas surrounded a glass tabletop, balanced on a stone dragon's back. More monster-themed artwork lined the walls.

A giant projection screen was available at the touch of a button. There was a kitchenette with a granite worktop and gold taps but no oven. The master bedroom included the most enormous bed she'd ever seen and an en-suite bathroom with a walk-in black granite shower. A second bedroom included two large single beds and another en-suite.

Chloe ran to the balcony and slid the two giant doors apart. A gust of wind caught her hair as she gleefully leaned over the balcony wall and looked down at the busy street forty floors below. She returned to the dining area. 'This is amazing. Can we live here?'

'We'd have to sell the Crown Jewels first,' Edith said.

Chloe and George looked at each other with a glint in their eyes.

'No,' Edith said.

Archie looked in the master bedroom. 'My room, I presume?'

'If you want to cover the cost, that's fine by me,' Edith said.

'I would not dream of depriving you of the experience. I'm sure one of these lovely couches will do me fine.'

George spotted a slim computer in the corner of the room at a black desk. There was a small printer underneath. 'It's got a computer!'

'It was an optional extra,' Edith said. 'Thought it might be handy. The blurb said the memory is securely wiped when you leave, or there's an option to do it yourself.'

George walked towards the machine. 'Awesome.'

'So, Archie,' Chloe said. 'What are all the supplies for?'

'We don't want the drone to fly too close, so we're going to make a parachute.'

George turned back and grimaced. 'I thought you were going to say that. But I'd hoped not.'

Archie shrugged. 'How hard can it be?'

'We'll soon find out,' George mumbled. When are we timing this for anyway? When's take off?'

'I've been thinking about that,' Edith said. We need to know they're safe. I think we should deliver them during the press conference.'

'Yes!' Chloe said. 'And then the whole world will know that they're back.'

'Fine,' George said. 'I'll see what I can find out about parachute design on the computer.'

'And I'll try to improve the fake jewels,' Chloe said.

Edith headed for the coffee-making facilities. 'I guess I'll help with the parachute... once I've had a coffee, of course!'

'And I've got to do some work on the car,' Archie said. 'But maybe I should leave that until later when the car park's quieter. Maybe one of you could help me attach the dark film to the car windows first?'

'Oh, Archie!' Chloe exclaimed suddenly. 'Before you do anything, I want to try something—an experiment.'

Archie looked nervous. 'Okay.'

'You know we were talking about Jack—that he must have got one of your hairs on him?'

'Yes...'

'I was thinking. Maybe we don't need your hair once we've spent enough time with you. Otherwise, why could Jack see you?'

Edith and George looked over, curious.

Chloe looked at Archie and removed the locket from her neck.

'Well?' Archie said.

Chloe wobbled a bit. Then she squinted. 'You've gone blurry.'

'Maybe you should leave it a bit longer,' Edith said.

Chloe held her hand up. 'No, it's okay....'

They waited.

Chloe opened her eyes more. 'You're becoming clearer.'

Finally, she smiled. 'I can see you, Archie.'

Archie smiled back at her. 'Really?' And then a bigger smile. 'Good.'

Edith looked down at the hair attached to her arm. 'I'll leave it a little longer.'

George nodded. 'And me.'

CHAPTER 37

MASTERS WAS AT HIS work desk when his phone rang. 'Masters,' he said, answering the phone. It was a colleague.

'Yeah, high Eddie, thought I should let you know we've had a reporter on the phone. The paper received a call from a man who saw a toy bear in the back of a car and then apparently lost time. Thought you might be interested. A woman in her thirties and two children returned to the car with a load of shopping shortly after.'

'What's the reporter's angle?'

'They're connecting the gap in time to the theft of the Crown Jewels. It's rubbish, of course. You know reporters—making connections when there's none to be made.'

'Quite,' Masters said. 'And where did this happen?'

'Top level of the multi-storey car park at that new shopping centre, The Landing. You know the one. Full of designer gear, open all hours. Claim they sell everything.'

'I know it. Anything else?'

'Nope, that was it.'

'Okay, thanks for the info.' Masters grabbed his jacket and headed out.

Masters pulled into the shopping centre car park and drove in circles to the top floor. He parked, looked around, and got the lift down to the shopping concourse. It was a grand place—full of modern art, expensive-looking sculptures and posh eateries.

He looked in a shop window of a clothing outlet. A bored junior sales assistant sat behind a desk, looking out. She had a good view of the main thoroughfare, so Masters entered the shop, approached the girl, smiled, and showed his badge. 'Afternoon. I'm looking for a family. They may have been here earlier and could be in trouble.' He took out the folded photo from his jacket pocket.

She examined the photo. 'Yes, I saw them. The lady came in here. She bought a charcoal blazer from the sale rack. Looked like they were on a bit of a shopping spree.'

Masters screwed his face up. *Shopping spree* wasn't the words he wanted to hear.

'Haven't seen them since, I'm afraid.'

'Do you recall what they were carrying?'

'It was all bagged up. Oh, I remember they bought a curtain pole.'

'Really? Do you have CCTV? Their shopping may give some clue to their intentions.'

'I doubt it,' the girl said. 'Apart from the curtain pole, you couldn't see what was in the bags.' She fetched a card from behind the counter. 'Here. I don't have access to the CCTV footage; you'd need to speak to my manager. She's not here, but her number is on the card.'

'Thanks. Did they say anything while they were with you?'

'Not that I recall.'

'And how did they seem?'

'Alright. A bit nervy, maybe.'

'Okay, thanks for your time.'

The girl smiled. 'You're welcome.'

Masters asked questions in a few more shops but learnt nothing new—it seemed that not all retail staff were overly interested in their customers' purchases. And if he demanded CCTV footage from every store, he'd be watching it until Christmas and probably still learn nothing useful.

He returned to his car. One thing was obvious—they were spending, which meant they had money. Had they sold the jewels to someone? His head fell onto the steering wheel as he considered his next move. If he told his colleagues and boss the truth, they'd think he was insane. They'd laugh him off the force.

Masters returned to the station. All he could do was go through the motions—pretend he didn't know who stole the Crown Jewels. And then he'd sleep on it. Maybe things would look different in the morning—maybe Archie and his new friends would do the honourable thing and return the jewels. If not... he had some difficult explaining to do.

CHAPTER 38

MORNING ARRIVED FAR QUICKER than Masters would have liked. He washed, dressed, and dished out cereal, which he gave up on after half a bowl.

A half-hour later, he pulled into the police station car park and sat there, thoughts rattling around his mind. How could he convince his boss that a sentient toy bear was responsible for one of the biggest heists ever committed? He called Edith again, but the number was still unobtainable. Masters massaged his temples, took a deep breath and headed inside.

He stood at the Chief Inspector's door, closed his eyes and gave a quick knock.

'Come in,' an authoritative voice barked, and Masters shuffled in and took a seat on the other side of the desk from his boss.

'Morning Eddie. Got your press release?'

'Yes, sir.' He pulled a copy out of his pocket and passed it across. As his boss read, Masters fidgeted self-consciously. He looked around the room. Framed photos and awards celebrated his boss's career.

'Something bothering you, Eddie?'

'No sir,' Masters said. 'Well... maybe, sir.'

'Spit it out then.'

Masters took a moment. 'I think Edith and her family may have had something to do with the theft.'

The Inspector looked up. 'Haven't we already been through this?'

'They're missing and... I need more time.' Masters tried to look calm. Once he'd captured Archie and friends and returned the jewels, he'd tell his boss everything. But for now, that wasn't an option. The Chief Inspector would never believe him.

'That's it?' his boss asked.

'They were seen shopping at that new place—The Landing. Edith gave the impression she was broke. Who goes shopping in a designer outlet when they have no money? Unless, of course, they've come into money, maybe sold something valuable....'

'Hardly conclusive evidence, is it?'

Masters broke eye contact as he considered how much more he could say without sounding insane.

The Chief Inspector was watching him. He slapped a meaty hand down on the table. 'Eddie. Stop holding back and tell me what you know!'

Masters dug into his jacket pocket, pulled out the photo of Edith with her family and placed it on the desk. 'We need to find her, and then I'll have your answers.'

The Chief Inspector looked at the photo. 'And you can't give me any more information to support your theory that this lady is responsible?'

'I'm not sure she is responsible... but I believe she's involved.'

'And she's gone missing?'

'Yes, sir. Just give me a few hours to track them down.'

The Chief Inspector regarded Masters with an analytical eye. 'I don't like this, and I'm sure you're holding back, but you've done good work in the past, so I'll grant you some leeway.'

'Thank you,' Masters said and reached out to retrieve the photo.

His boss pulled the photo towards himself. 'I don't think so.'

Masters hovered, looking for some reason to get the photo back, but none came.

'I'll give you your few hours, but if this woman knows something, we need to release her picture to the media. Unless there's anything else you feel you should tell me?'

Masters hesitated, but Edith and her family hadn't made contact—what else was he supposed to do? 'No, sir, I'm sure you're right.'

'Okay, Eddie. Now go and find her.'

Masters nodded, dragged himself up and left.

An hour later, Masters was sat at his desk phoning hotels and B&Bs when it occurred to him that if Edith had come into money, it might be worth trying a few of the more upmarket hotels.

He still felt conflicted. It made no sense. Why did Archie hand himself in, if not to return the jewels? That's assuming he didn't imagine him. But no one, not Edith, Archie, George or Chloe, had attempted to contact him. What hurt was that he had wanted to help them. But he had a job to do, so he ran a new search, concentrating on London's more upmarket hotels.

CHAPTER 39

A SHRILL ALARM WOKE Chloe up. The noise startled her until she remembered where she was—the Kraken Hotel. She silenced the alarm and looked across to her brother's bed. He was either asleep or doing his best to ignore the world.

Chloe grabbed her clothes and entered the ensuite bathroom, where she chose a mandarin and grapefruit shower gel from the available selection. The shower was amazing, hot with plenty of pressure. But despite feeling fresh and smelling good, it didn't help calm the rapidly encroaching feeling of dread she felt. She grabbed a plump towel from a shelf, dried herself, dressed, and cleaned her teeth. As she emerged from the bathroom, George wordlessly slipped past her. 'Morning,' Chloe said.

'Morning,' George grunted.

Chloe went into the lounge area. Mum was already up and nursing a coffee. They said their good mornings, and Chloe noticed a quiver in her mum's voice. It was going to be a long day. She continued to the sofa and sat down opposite Archie.

Archie waved at her.

Chloe struggled for a second as her view of Archie came into focus. 'Hi,' she said and stared at him. It took a few seconds for her brain to catch up with reality. But reality was weird, so she got up and walked towards the balcony doors. She pulled them apart and stepped outside to let the breeze blow through her freshly washed hair. She leaned on the balcony and looked across London's landscape.

After a minute, someone joined her.

'Are you okay?' Archie asked.

Chloe let out a nervous laugh. 'This is all mad. You, the Crown Jewels, being here. All of it.'

Archie had the grace to look guilty. 'I'll do everything I can to make things right. Can I ask a favour?'

Chloe continued staring at the London skyline for a moment. 'Sure.'

'I can't see over the balcony.'

'Oh,' Chloe said. She turned and gently picked him up. 'You're heavy!'

'It's all muscle.' He looked across the sprawling architecture, from ultra-modern glass towers to fifteenth-century churches. 'Wow.'

'It's pretty cool,' Chloe agreed.

'It's amazing.'

She struggled to hold Archie but clung on a little longer.

'Although planting a few more trees wouldn't hurt,' Archie said.

Chloe lowered Archie. 'Why did you do it?'

Archie looked blank for a moment. 'I knew I had to do something big to prove I was alive. Anything else, you'd have ignored it or blamed each other. Like the note. You thought George wrote it.'

'But the *Crown Jewels?*'

'I'm not sure I really understand material things. Perhaps it's part of my... programming. I think that's the word you use these days.'

'Programming?' Chloe repeated, wondering what Archie was.

'Not literally. Or at least, I don't believe so.'

Chloe still didn't understand.

Archie sighed. 'I had a home once, although not for long. I just wanted that again. And what chance do I have if no one knows I'm alive?' He looked down. 'Although I guess I've mucked that up.'

Chloe looked into the distance. 'I still don't agree with what you did.'

'I know.'

'Chloe!' Edith called.

Chloe headed back in, followed by Archie, and they returned to the settees.

'We should eat,' Edith said. 'Archie, do you eat?'

Archie shook his head.

'Then how do you get energy?'

'I don't know—although when you opened my box, I think the light woke me up.'

'Hmm.' Edith turned to Chloe. 'It's a buffet. Are you coming?'

Chloe thought for a second. 'Can you get me something? I'll keep Archie company.'

'Sure,' Edith said. She called George, who wandered out of the bedroom, drying his hair.

'Morning. Do you want to go down for the breakfast buffet?'

'Cool,' George said, 'Let's go.' He threw the towel on the small kitchen worktop and headed for the door.

'Er, towel,' Edith said.

George gave the towel a confused look, folded it neatly and put it back on the worktop.

'Not quite what I meant, but let's go.'

The restaurant was called Dante's Cavern. Two stone demons stood on either side of the entrance holding stone platters displaying stylish menus. The cavern looked like it was carved from stone. Ribbons of red lava ran in cracks up the walls. A white piano with bony outgrowths sat on a platform at the far end.

Edith and George picked up two large plates and loaded up a selection of breakfast items. At one point, Edith caught the attention of a waitress. 'I don't suppose you have a container I could use for my daughter? She wasn't quite ready to come down.'

'Of course,' the woman said and found a polystyrene container and some plastic cutlery.

They piled up their plates and the container and sat to eat.

Edith admired her surroundings. 'In any other circumstance, this would be pretty cool.'

'It's still cool, Mum,' George said and shovelled a forkful of beans and fried potatoes into his mouth.

She looked around. 'Yeah, but let's not forget why we're here.'

'As if,' George said between mouthfuls.

Edith was about to eat when she was distracted by a large TV screen in an alcove. It was playing the morning news. She squinted, trying to make out a familiar figure on the screen. 'Oh...'

She dropped her fork and swore.

George looked at his mum in surprise, and she pointed at the TV behind him.

'...police would like to speak to this woman in connection with the theft of the Crown Jewels. She is likely travelling with two children, aged twelve and fourteen. If you see her, please call us on this number....'

George choked and nervously looked around. 'Mum, that's you!'

'Ssshh,' she said and guiltily looked down at her plate.

'I don't think anyone's watching,' George whispered.

Edith nodded. 'Let's finish our food.' She knocked the salt cellar over as she reached for her coffee.

George raised his eyebrows. 'Mum!'

Chloe was examining her fake Crown Jewels when the door burst open. She jumped, very nearly ripping the cardboard crown in half. She held a hand to her heart as Mum and George tumbled inside.

'They're onto us!' Edith hissed whilst slapping down Chloe's breakfast in the polystyrene container.

'How?' Chloe cried.

'Detective Masters, he must have cracked. I've just seen my face on the news! And I thought he trusted us....'

'To be fair, we didn't trust him,' George observed.

'I left him a note!' Edith said defensively.

'He may not have told them everything,' Archie said from one of the sofas. 'I mean, who'd believe him? Even I don't understand it.'

Edith dropped down on the sofa opposite Archie.

'Do you think we'll have time to see this through?' Archie asked.

'I don't know.'

'We're almost there, Mum,' Chloe said. 'We worked half the night. Archie spent hours inside the car doing... well, whatever he was doing. Just a little longer.'

Edith let out a pained sigh. 'I reserved the hotel room using my sister's name. It was her card, so I had little choice. It may buy us some time... but this is all getting out of control.'

'Don't worry,' Archie said, 'It'll work out.'

Edith turned on Archie, her eyes blazing. 'Don't worry! You stole the Crown Jewels, and we covered it up. And if that detective has told them everything, they'll be here soon enough to take you away.'

Archie took a step backwards.

Edith looked away, composed herself, and turned back to Archie. 'Sorry.'

'It's okay.'

The hotel room descended into silence. Even the hum of traffic couldn't break through the triple-glazed balcony doors.

George smiled. 'Well, let them take him!'

Chloe looked at George in disgust. 'George!'

Edith sat there, looking numb.

'Not our Archie,' George said. 'Didn't you tell that detective you could get a replica of Archie on eBay?'

Edith sat up slightly.

Chloe's eyes twinkled. 'That's a pretty good idea....'

'Thanks.'

'We may need to dye its hair a little darker,' Archie said.

'Tea,' Chloe said. 'I remember using it as a dye to make paper look old at primary school.'

Edith rubbed her face. It took a moment before she spoke. 'Okay... I better get on with it, I guess.' She dragged herself off the couch and over to the PC. With a few key presses, she brought up eBay. After a few more, she found an Archie bear among the listings. 'The local one is still available.'

'Do it, Mum,' Chloe said.

Edith took a deep breath. 'I'm going to owe my sister so much money.'

'If it keeps us all out of prison, she won't care, Mum,' Chloe said. 'And besides, what's a couple of thousand to her—a week's wages?'

'I'll have to tell her everything when she gets back. Is that okay with you, Archie?'

'Sure,' Archie said, seemingly without concern.

Edith didn't quite share his optimism, but she phoned the seller and, after a brief discussion, agreed to buy the replica Archie for fifty pounds less than the advertised price. She printed out the details and folded them in half. 'I'd better get going,' she said, wobbling a little on her feet as she stood up.

George looked on with concern. 'Mum, your face is on the news. You're like, *famous*, and not in a good way. And I'm not sure you should drive right now....'

'Ask Hasani,' Chloe suggested.

'The bellhop?'

'I think he likes you after that twenty-pound note you gave him.'

Edith raised her eyebrows, gave a crooked smile and phoned reception, who told her that Hasani would be right with them. She turned to George. 'There's an ATM in the lobby. Do you think you could run down and get five hundred pounds out? The pin is one-five-zero-one.'

'Sure,' George said, grabbed the card from her and charged out of the door.

Meanwhile, they raced around, moving their purchases—especially the drone—to the bedroom. A few minutes later, there was a knock at the door.

Edith opened the door to the bellhop. 'Hasani, thank you for coming.'

Hasani gave a broad smile. 'You ask; I appear. I am at your disposal.'

'Could you pick something up for me? It's local.'

'Of course, madam.'

'You won't get in trouble?'

'Not at all; there are plenty of us. All part of the service.'

'Great,' Edith said with a relieved smile and gave him the printout. 'It's a teddy bear. It's hard to explain, but we need it immediately. And I'd prefer it if you didn't mention it to anyone.'

'Discretion is my middle name, as long as I am not assisting a crime—or at least nothing serious.' He laughed.

George burst back into the room with a fistful of notes.

'Perfect timing!' Edith said and took the cash.

'Don't worry,' Edith assured Hasani, 'you're committing no crime, but as I said, keep it quiet.'

Hasani looked a little suspicious.

'There's fifty in it for you.'

He beamed. 'It would be my absolute pleasure, discretion guaranteed.'

Edith gave him the cash. 'I'll let the seller know you're coming.'

Hasani looked at the address on the print. 'I have a moped. I can be there in fifteen minutes.'

'Thank you.'

'My pleasure,' Hasani said.

'Oh, and I may need you to drop something off at the post office later if you wouldn't mind,' Edith added.

'Not a problem, Madam.' Hasani gave a quick nod and left the room.

Edith glanced at her watch. 'I guess we should get on with things. Don't forget the gloves!'

Archie looked at his paws.

'Okay, not you,' Edith said.

Chloe and George retrieved their stuff from the bedroom. Archie stretched the material they'd bought out on the floor. Yesterday, they'd cut it into a large circle, and around the edge, they'd attached twelve small eyelets with a length of twine tied to each.

George laughed. 'What is that supposed to be!' He pointed to a face drawn on the parachute—two enormous eyes with lopsided pupils, a piggish nose and a daft grin.

'A distraction. I'd rather the press took pictures of a silly face than the drone,' Edith explained.

'Okay, that makes some sense, I guess. I'll double-check the altitude we need on the PC.'

'And I still need to spray the fake jewels,' Chloe said.

'Try not to paint the floor gold!' George warned.

Chloe furrowed her eyebrows. 'Okay, bossy pants.' She found a roll of brown paper from their recent purchases and laid a large sheet on the floor, just in case.

Archie followed George to the PC and watched him. 'So, you can ask this device any question, and it will answer it?'

'Yep,' George said. 'As long as there's a proper answer. It won't tell you the lottery results for next week, but if you want to know who was top of the charts on the day you were born or how big the sun is, then easy.'

'That's the most incredible thing I've ever heard.'

'I suppose it is. I've never given it much thought. And you don't even need a big computer; you can do it on Mum's phone.'

Archie looked stunned. 'And anyone can do this?'

'Anyone with an internet connection and some sort of computer. Two-thirds of the world, maybe.'

'Two-thirds of the planet has access to unlimited knowledge?'

'Yep.'

'Wow,' Archie said. 'What an amazing time to be alive.'

CHAPTER 40

DETECTIVE MASTERS PUT THE phone down and sighed. He leaned back and surveyed the office. Everyone appeared busy except PC John Leary, who was laughing at something on his monitor with another officer. Typical.

'Leary,' Masters shouted. 'Come here, please. And bring—'

'Jacobs, sir,' he said as they walked over.

'Yes, of course. I need your help.' Masters pointed at his list of hotel names. 'I'll never get through these on my own, and I must prepare for the press conference. But Edith and her family could be staying at one of these.'

'And if the hotel won't divulge that information over the phone, sir?' Jacobs asked.

'Improvise.'

'And what should we do if we find her while you're at the press conference?' Leary queried.

Masters frowned and wondered whether this was going to get complicated. But it was getting late, and the calls were taking too long. PC Leary—who was usually rather irritating—looked eager to prove himself, so he continued. 'Bring them in for questioning. If they refuse, arrest them for suspected involvement in the theft of the Crown Jewels.'

He remembered that taking Archie could be problematic and exhaled slowly.

'What is it, sir?' Leary asked.

There were a couple of newspaper clippings on Masters' desk. He pressed one into each of the men's hands. 'The press are linking the incident at Potters Fields to the robbery. Sightseers said they froze after seeing a toy bear. The soldiers at Jewel House also reported losing time. And given that we found hair used in teddy bear construction at the crime site, who knows? Maybe they are connected.'

Masters felt a twinge of guilt as the officers skimmed the clippings. But what choice did he have? He couldn't tell them a toy bear stole the Crown Jewels, and besides, there was still time for Archie and friends to make contact.

The men passed the clippings back.

Leary seemed unusually quiet and was looking rather pale. He ran an anxious hand through his slick, blond hair but said nothing.

Masters typed away at his PC and then twisted the monitor to show an image of Archie. 'This is Archie; this is the bear they apparently saw. If you see him, bring him in as well.'

Jacobs looked confused, but PC Leary—whom he'd expected to say something stupid—was silent. Masters was not sure what to make of it. 'Anyway, you've read the clippings. Just remain open-minded. And if you see Archie, cuff him, just in case!'

Masters looked at Jacob's bemused face. Who could blame him? 'You know what—forget it. Just call the hotels and let me know if you find something. Leave a message if you need to.'

'No, we'll do it, sir,' PC Leary said.

'Err, yeah. Leave it to us, sir.' Jacobs agreed.

Masters handed each officer a list of numbers. 'Oh, one more thing. If you find Archie, you'll need this....'

He took out a small bag with Archie's hairs inside, ripped off a couple of pieces of tape and stuck a hair on each officer's forearm.

The officers looked at their arms and then back at Masters.

'It'll take too long to explain, but it may stop you from losing time. Don't remove that tape, okay?' He tapped the newspaper clippings on his desk. 'I know how this all sounds. Read these properly, stay open-minded and don't mention this to anyone.'

'It's fine, sir,' Leary said and walked off with his list.

Jacobs gave a slight nod and followed his colleague.

Masters watched Leary. He had fully expected the cocky young officer to make all sorts of wisecracks, but nothing. Something wasn't right.

CHAPTER 41

CHLOE SAT ON THE floor, admiring her work. The fake jewels were far more convincing now that she'd sprayed the 'metal' parts gold. Plus, Mum had picked up some air-dry modelling clay during their shopping trip, which was great for adding a few fiddly bits. She held them up proudly. 'What do you think, Mum?'

'Are those the real ones?' Edith asked, her smile not quite reaching her eyes.

'Haha,' Chloe said, but she was pleased with how they'd turned out. She picked up the brown paper and was thankful that the carpet underneath was still its original colour. She looked back at her family working. To her surprise, they'd become a team.

George had a hairdryer and was drying the fake Archie after using tea to stain the bear's fur. And he'd made a decent job of it.

Edith and Archie were huddled around printed instructions for folding a parachute. They repeatedly folded the material until it resembled a pizza slice with twelve strong lengths of twine, then referred back to the diagram. 'I get it,' Archie said and completed further folds in a concertina fashion until he had a small square package.

Chloe moved over to one of the sofas to watch the final touches. The jewels were now protected with bubble wrap and taped to a cardboard base. Cling film covered it all to aid aerodynamics. They just needed to attach the parachute.

Archie tied the first length of twine to the cardboard base whilst Edith nibbled at her nails.

'It'll work,' Archie said and gave a reassuring smile.

'I hope so.' Edith started tying the next one.

Over the next few minutes, Edith and Archie connected the rest of the twine. It was a fiddly job, especially whilst wearing rubber gloves. Each length of twine had to be the same length. Otherwise, the package would hang lopsidedly and force the drone off course.

Finally, they made noises of approval and then carefully hung the box from a remotely operated claw-like mechanism on the drone's underside.

'Looking good,' Chloe said and watched as they lifted the drone to see how the package hung.

Edith gave a slight nervous smile.

Archie added a bit of masking tape between the bottom of the drone and the top of the parachute. In theory, the masking tape would pull on the parachute enough to help it open as it dropped.

Edith nodded as she assessed their work. 'It just needs its skirt and legs, and we're done.'

George turned. 'Sorry?'

'You'll see.'

Archie climbed onto the couch next to Chloe and gave a tired sigh. 'It's almost as hard returning them as it was taking them.'

Chloe gave Archie a playful shove. Archie up-righted himself, and Chloe chuckled. Archie smiled back. For a moment, it was almost like he was one of the family.

George brought over the replica of Archie and put him down next to the real Archie.

Archie turned to his look-alike. 'This is weird.'

'You're better looking than the fake one,' Chloe said.

Archie coughed politely. 'Over here, Chloe!'

She smiled sweetly and turned from the replica to Archie.

'Right,' Archie said. 'As much fun as this is, I think it's time. Edith, would you mind taking me down to the car?' He jumped off the couch and climbed into the suitcase.

'Good luck!' Chloe said.

'You sure about this, Archie?' George asked.

'Absolutely. Remember, I'm not a toy bear. I'm an intelligent being, the same as any of you.'

Edith sat wide-eyed and shaky.

George noticed his mum was struggling. 'Don't worry, Mum. It's still better if you're not seen. I'll take Archie down.'

'Are you sure you can hold him?'

'Of course.' He went to the suitcase and looked down at Archie's crumpled-up body. 'Ready, Archie?'

Archie nodded, and George gently closed the case and tried it out for weight. 'It's fine.'

Chloe decided that now and then, her brother was okay.

Edith chucked the car keys over, which George tried to catch one-handed, but they slid through his fingers. He cleared his throat as he bent down to pick them up. 'Okay, ready.'

'Oh, you'll need these,' Edith said. She clambered up and found a pair of wellington boots, each with a large block of wood screwed and taped to the bottom. She put them into the sports bag and slung it over George's shoulder.

'You good?' Edith asked.

'Yeah.' George adjusted the strap a little and gave his mum a nod that he was okay. 'Right, err... Grab a coffee. I will return.'

Chloe gave a crooked smile. 'Is that your catchphrase?'

'No!'

'Good. It needs some work.'

George left carrying Archie, and Edith buried her head in her hands in mild panic.

Chloe returned to working on the fake jewels. Meanwhile, Edith excused herself for a laydown.

George returned thirty minutes later, and Edith emerged from the bedroom. 'Any problems?' she asked.

Chloe could see her mum was getting more nervous by the minute and hoped George said something positive for once.

'We attached the film to black out the windows. The car almost looks cool.'

Chloe breathed a silent sigh of relief.

'Of course, that won't prevent our imminent imprisonment,' George added.

Chloe glared at George.

He caught her look. 'I'm joking, Mum. Everything is going to be fine.'

At the hotel's reception desk, a phone rang. A smartly dressed young woman picked it up. 'Kraken Hotel, how can I help?'

'Good afternoon, my name's PC Leary. Could you put me through to Edith Moran's room, please? We had a call from her but got cut off.'

The receptionist checked her records. 'We don't have an Edith Moran, sorry.'

'It could be booked under her sister's name—Carole Webb?'

'Webb... err yes, we have a Carole Webb.'

'Mid-thirties—two children?' Leary asked.

'Yes, that sounds about right.'

'Excellent. On second thoughts, don't put me through. It's probably better if we talk in person. Thanks for your help. I'll be with you shortly.'

The receptionist lowered the phone. She looked worried that she'd divulged confidential information, but then the phone rang again, so she took a breath and moved on to the next call.

CHAPTER 42

PC LEARY AND PC Jacobs rushed from the station and jumped into a police car. Leary was unusually quiet as he buckled up.

'You okay, mate?' Jacobs asked.

Leary ran a hand through his blond hair and started the engine. He nodded silently, staring forwards.

Jacobs looked at his arm. 'Do you know why we have a hair taped to our forearms?'

The car was silent.

'Are you ignoring me?' Jacobs asked.

PC Leary looked at him. He held his gaze for an uncomfortable amount of time. 'I've seen him.'

'Seen who?'

'Yesterday, I was stationed by Edith Moran's house. Something knocked on the window. I turned, and I saw... I saw the bear that Masters showed us in the station. I saw Archie. It was only for a fraction of a second—a millisecond—and then he was gone. But it was like time stopped.'

'You're having me on.'

'I'm not.'

'I know what you're like.'

'Suit yourself,' Leary said, 'but I'm telling you the truth. Buckle up.'

Tyres squealing, Leary raced from the station car park.

Jacobs dug his fingers into his legs as he was forced back into his seat. 'Easy, mate! We're no use to anyone if we're dead!'

'I've taken the advanced driving course.'

'I don't care what you've taken,' Jacobs said as he double-checked his seat belt.

CHAPTER 43

CHLOE, GEORGE, AND EDITH carried the drone onto the balcony and positioned it over two chairs. A strong breeze rattled the machine, and they shared a nervous look.

'It's fine,' Chloe said. She looked around to ensure their balcony wasn't overlooked, then returned her attention to the Crown Jewels. They were attached to a cardboard base and hung from a clasp under the drone. They'd secured thin red material around the outside and drawn seams to make it look like a skirt. And they'd hung a pair of long stripy black and yellow socks filled with bubble wrap from the underside.

Chloe sniggered. 'It looks daft.'

'Good,' Edith said. 'The more people are distracted from the actual drone, the less chance there is of anyone identifying it.' She put a hand to her heart and took a deep breath.

George looked at his watch. 'It's time.'

Chloe peered over the balcony. Traffic was heaving, but none of the human dots below appeared to be looking up at them. 'All clear, Mum.'

Edith grabbed the control box. It had an attached strap which she slipped around her neck, but she still gripped the controls like they were alive.

She stood there, not moving.

Chloe nudged her mum's arm. 'Mum?'

Edith slowly shook her head. She looked pale.

'Mum, we need to go now,' George urged.

'I'm not sure about this....'

Edith's breathing sounded strange, quick choppy breaths like she was running out of air.

George stepped in front of her and lifted the strap from around her neck.

'What... what are you doing?' Edith said breathlessly.

'We both know how to fly this drone, remember?'

'Y-Yes, but...'

George got comfortable with the control box and powered up the drone. Four pairs of blades, a pair on each of the four arms, spun into action. He pushed the throttle forward, and the drone rose. Its whine increased as the lines became taught. George applied a little more throttle, and the package left the ground with a shudder.

Chloe shrieked with delight, then grabbed one of the now free chairs and pulled it back for her mum. 'Sit down, Mum.'

Edith did as she was told.

George allowed the two joysticks to centre, and the drone hovered in front of them. He eased the right joystick forward. The drone tipped down and moved over the bustling streets far below. He increased the throttle with the left joystick, and the Crown Jewels began their flight to the Tower of London.

Chloe peered at the screen built into the control box. After a minute, she turned away. The view of the buildings passing below made her head spin. Or maybe it was just the fact that they'd be there in a few minutes that turned her stomach.

CHAPTER 44

MASTERS SHUFFLED TOWARDS A podium erected in front of Jewel House within the grounds of the Tower of London. A crowd of eager reporters—fifty, perhaps more—shuffled around and pointed cameras and microphones at him. His stomach turned.

He took a sip of water and cleared his throat. 'Good morning. Thank you all for coming.'

The sea of reporters waited expectantly.

Masters drew out a speech. 'My name is Detective Eddie Masters. On behalf of The Metropolitan Police, I'm authorised to share what we know about the theft of the Crown Jewels.

Masters brushed his hair back. He cleared his throat again and drank more water. *Why hadn't Edith contacted him? Or Chloe, or George, or even Archie... He'd trusted them. And they'd thrown it back in his face.*

The press looked impatient.

'There will be a dedicated number at the bottom of the screen throughout. Please contact us if you have any information which may help recover the Crown Jewels and bring the perpetrators to justice.'

Masters looked at his speech.

'On Wednesday evening, just after six, the thief or thieves walked into Jewel House. That's the b—'

'How did they walk into a heavily guarded building?' a reporter shouted.

'I will take questions at the end.' Masters replied sternly.

Another reporter put his hand up. Masters ignored him. 'As I was saying, they walked into Jewel House—that's the building behind me. The soldiers on guard have no recollection of the event. Everyone we spoke to reports losing time as though they were unconscious—'

'Come on, detective,' a reporter shouted, 'give us something real.'

Masters looked helpless for a moment.

'It's strange, I grant you. The CCTV cameras froze throughout the robbery; however, a security robot put up some sort of fight.'

Masters drank more water. *Why had Archie and his friends done this? And what were their plans now?*

One of the press reporters coughed loudly, and Masters continued. 'Unfortunately, the robot failed to stop the thieves, who left behind two items: A note saying *just borrowed.* And we found a fistful of hair which we believe the robot tore out during the robbery. We've analysed the hair and have identified it's used in teddy bear construction.' A confused murmur ran through the crowd of reporters. Masters pressed on.

'I can confirm that three items were stolen: The Imperial State Crown, the Sovereign Orb and the Sovereign Sceptre with Cross.'

Naming the treasures aloud made it worse, made it more real. *The priceless objects had been in his house. What was he thinking? He'd given them enough time... it was time to tell the press about Archie.*

The press sensed the change in his demeanour and waited eagerly, although some were now looking around.

'We have now traced those hairs to—'

The reporters looked skywards.

Masters followed their gaze. There was something in the sky. A high-pitched whine accompanied it. He turned to a soldier who was already looking through his rifle scope. 'Soldier, don't fire! What do you see?'

'Looks like a drone, sir. It's carrying something....'

'What?'

'I'm not sure. It's weird. Whatever the package is, it seems to be wearing a skirt, and there's a pair of legs dangling from the centre....'

'Legs?'

'Not real legs. Stuffed socks or tights,' the soldier said.

The whir of the drone's blades grew louder.

'It's covered in bubble wrap,' the soldier continued. 'There's something long sticking out, like a staff.'

Or a sceptre, Masters thought.

The Press excitedly aimed their cameras at the legs swinging from the parcel suspended high above them.

Some of the police officers were getting worried.

A soldier approached Detective Masters. 'I think we need to take it down, sir.'

'What if it's the jewels? Do you think they'll survive that sort of drop?'

'Human life is my priority, sir. It could be a threat. We don't know for sure what it's carrying.'

The Soldier looked through his scope at the drone.

'Can you see anything that could be a danger to us?' Masters asked.

'No, but it's pretty strange, sir. We should act now.'

CHAPTER 45

PC LEARY CAUGHT SIGHT of the Kraken Hotel as the police car sped through London. The building's imposing presence against the skyline spurred him on. He overtook another vehicle and accelerated towards an oncoming lorry.

At the last second, he yanked the wheel left and pulled back into his lane.

Jacobs breathed out. 'Next time, I'm driving!'

'We can't allow them to leave,' Leary said. 'This is all to do with the bear, I'm telling you.'

'You're talking crazy,'

'You read the article. People froze after seeing him. It has to be connected.'

'And the hairs?' Jacobs said, looking at his arm.

'Masters said something about preventing us from losing time. Maybe we'll be able to talk to him...'

'Talk to who?'

'Archie. Haven't you listened to anything I've been saying?'

'You think you can talk to a *teddy bear*? You're losing it, pal.'

'Let's just get there.'

'Fine. And remember, we're just supposed to bring them in.'

'Right,' Leary said with a steely look.

Jacobs shook his head.

CHAPTER 46

CHLOE AND GEORGE STOOD on the fortieth-floor balcony of the Kraken Hotel and watched the small screen in the drone's control box. The drone hovered over the press, standing four hundred feet below. Edith forced herself up from the chair and joined them.

'Is that Masters down there?' Edith said, pointing at the podium in front of the press, but then the angle changed, and he was gone.

Chloe nodded. 'I think it was... I wonder what he's thinking?'

'Nothing good.'

'Altitude is good,' George said. He checked the wind speed and direction. 'We just need to fly west a bit.' He slid the right-hand joystick to the left, and the drone obeyed. 'I think that'll do it.' He allowed the controls to centre so that the drone hovered. 'All agreed?'

Chloe and Edith nodded. They were too nervous to talk.

'Here goes then.' He pressed a button on the box marked *release*.

Nothing happened.

'No!' Edith gasped.

'What's happening?' Chloe cried.

'I.... I don't know,' George said. 'I need to try something. Mum, can you take over for a second?'

'What? Well... I....' She took a deep breath and nodded. 'Okay, give it to me.'

'Just fly in circles for a minute. Trust me!' He transferred the control box to his mum and ran back into the hotel room.

Masters was staring at the strange site above him when an officer approached. 'Good news, sir, we'll have a drone of our own here in the next few minutes.'

'Is it in the air now?' Masters asked.

'Well, no sir. We have to be in the line of sight. It's civil aviation regs.'

'So the drone is arriving by car?'

'Yes, sir, but it'll be in the air in minutes.'

Masters shook his head. 'Unbelievable. Does it have any military capabilities?'

'No, but it's equipped with a high-definition camera. If there are any identifying markings, we'll get them, and we may be able to force the other drone down.'

'Okay, good. All we need now is a flying car to deliver it.'

The officer paused.

'That was a joke.'

'Yes, sir. Sorry, sir.'

George ran back onto the hotel balcony with a slim knife and a small screwdriver. He loosened a couple of screws on the drone's control box and used the blade to pop the plastic cover off the section housing the release button.

A wire was loose inside. It was clearly supposed to attach to a terminal under the release button. George moved the wire back in place and got ready to press it down with the head of the screwdriver.

He checked the display. 'Ten metres east, Mum.'

She did as he asked.

'And the same, higher.'

Edith increased the throttle.

'Okay, looks good to me,' George said.

Chloe bounced up and down on the souls of her feet. 'Do it!'

George used the screwdriver and pressed the loose wire to the contact.

They all held their breath.

The drone released its package.

Edith rotated the camera in time to catch the chute opening, and they caught a glimpse of the press pointing their cameras to the sky.

'Yes!' Edith cried, clenching her fist.

George and Chloe cheered.

The huge, dorky face drawn onto the parachute stared back at them through the view screen.

'Get out of there, Mum,' Chloe urged.

She flew the drone higher, rotated it, and then sent it on a path towards the Thames.

'Do you want me to take it?' George asked his mum.

'No. I can do this.'

CHAPTER 47

As MASTERS WATCHED THE drone, there was a mechanical sound from above, and it released its package. He watched the parachute open. The weird cartoon face with the piggy nose rotated towards him. He squinted to take in the details and, for a second, doubted what he was seeing.

The press scrambled to shoot pictures as the parachute dropped.

Masters shook his head in wonder.

A senior officer pulled out his radio. 'Get as many cars out as you can. I need them to follow a drone leaving the Tower of London.' He looked flustered. 'Yes, I know cars can't fly, but it seems our own drone is delayed in traffic. Just do it!'

The reporters continued clicking as the package came to rest between them and the podium. The stuffed legs crumpled underneath, cushioning its landing.

Masters ran from the podium to the package. 'Everyone, back up, please!' The press obeyed, but not as far as he would have liked. He nervously peeled back the outer film and then pulled back the bubble wrap on the staff. The four hundred million pound diamond glittered under the sun. The Sovereign Sceptre was back. He let out a small 'yes' and clenched his fist in celebration. Then he looked to the sky and watched the drone fly to the horizon until it was just a dot. He let his head drop and closed his eyes as he took a moment to breathe again.

The noise of untold camera shutters and the clambering press forced Masters into action. 'Back up, please!' He folded up the parachute and scooped up the jewels.

Two soldiers flanked every move he made.

'Do you have anything to say, detective?' a reporter asked.

Masters climbed back onto the podium. 'It appears the Crown Jewels have been returned. Thank you for coming today. I am afraid that will be all for now.'

'Show us the Jewels!' a reporter shouted.

Masters smiled. Contaminating evidence with his fingerprints wouldn't go down well, and then a truly horrible thought occurred to him. At his house, he'd taken the Sovereign Sceptre from Edith. Were his prints on it? Had Edith wiped the jewels down? He couldn't be sure. How could he explain his prints on the sceptre? There was only one option.

Masters freed the sceptre from the packaging, took hold of the gold rod and raised it high in the air for the press to see. The diamond glittered for the cameras.

A couple of police officers' jaws dropped.

The press cheered and started taking photos. Masters smiled awkwardly at the cameras but knew his actions were unthinkable.

The Chief Inspector stormed towards him. *Here we go—sacked in front of the media.*

Masters' boss stopped inches from him. He peeled back the bubble wrap from the Imperial State Crown and Sovereign Orb, sidled up to Masters and lifted the treasures triumphantly into the air. The press cheered again and snapped more pictures.

Meanwhile, the police drone arrived above them, circled and then shot off in search of its target.

CHAPTER 48

CHLOE SPOKE INTO A mobile, which was on speakerphone. 'You there, Archie?'

'Here and ready,' Archie replied from his position on the side of the road in Edith's car.

Chloe checked the screen. 'The drone is a minute away. Get going!'

They heard a car engine starting. 'Leaving now,' Archie said through the speaker.

As Archie pulled away in Edith's car, a car horn honked loudly.

'Oops,' they heard Archie say. Edith closed her eyes in despair and then returned her attention to flying the drone. Their old Ford came into view on the controller's built-in view screen.

'We see you,' Chloe said into the phone.

Edith sent the drone into a dive.

Chloe leaned towards the phone. 'Slow down a little, Archie. We'll be at the tunnel in about ten seconds.'

They watched the screen as their car slowed and entered the tunnel. The drone swooped in behind, but the ground was approaching too quickly. Chloe closed her eyes as Edith pulled back, almost scraping the drone on the tarmac.

The car was only a couple of meters ahead. The windows were blacked out to prevent prying eyes, and the back seats were down. The rear window lay flat inside the car on a hinged arrangement. As the drone edged inside the vehicle, they glimpsed Archie in the driver's seat.

Edith nudged the left stick forward, and the drone flew into the back of the car, slamming into Archie's headrest. It came to a rest in a tilted position, and the blades slowed to a stop. 'Are you okay, Archie?' Edith said breathlessly into the phone.

They could see a bit of Archie through the drone's camera. Archie rubbed the back of his head. 'Just a bump, I'm fine!'

'How are the blocks holding up?'

'Still attached!'

They watched Archie pull a string attached to the roof, which they knew would cause the blacked-out rear window to snap back into its rightful place.

Edith put the control box down. She turned to Chloe and George, hardly daring to speak the words. Some colour returned to her features, and she smiled. 'I think we did it!'

Chloe and George both gave squeals of delight. Chloe held her hand up in the air, and Edith slapped her hand, followed by George. She spoke into the speakerphone. 'Good driving, Archie!'

'Thanks,' Archie said, his voice coming through the speaker.

'We'll see you later,' Edith said. 'And please don't get pulled over!'

'I'll do my best!'

Chloe grabbed the controls from her mum and ran to the front room. She placed the unit back in its polystyrene compartment in the original cardboard box, stuffed the remaining space with any incriminating evidence, and then wrapped it in brown paper. She wrote her name and address on the top of the box.

There was a loud knock on the door.

Chloe's heart hammered in her chest.

George jumped and turned to the door.

For a moment, no one moved.

The knock came again.

Edith went to the door, took a breath, and pulled it open. 'Hasani!' She said with relief. Perfect timing.

The bellhop smiled happily, 'You said ten past three, and so at ten past three, I am here. Anything for my favourite guest!'

'Thank you. You're a marvel. This needs to go immediately!'

She pulled out fifty pounds in notes and passed them to him. 'Keep the change. And thank you. I can rely on your discretion?'

'Of course, madam,' he said and gratefully pocketed the money. 'The hotel values its clients' privacy.'

Hasani left with the box.

Chloe grinned. 'We really did it, Mum.'

'That was some cool flying, Mum,' George said.

Edith smiled. 'Why, thank you. You weren't bad yourself!'

They all jumped as another knock, this time more urgent, hammered at the door.

The family turned to stare at it.

'Ms Moran, could you open up, please? It's the police.'

'Oh,' Edith said.

Chloe switched on the TV, hoping it would make things appear more normal. 'It's okay, Mum.' She went to the hotel room door and opened it. Two police officers stood waiting, and Chloe let out a small gasp—the blond officer was the one Archie had frozen in the car outside their house.

'Are you okay?' PC Jacobs asked.

Chloe recovered. 'Yes, sorry. Can I help you?'

'Can we speak to your mum, please?'

Edith appeared at the door. She also recognised the officer but composed herself quickly. 'Hello, officers. How can I help you?'

'Are you aware that your face has been on the news?' PC Leary asked.

'The News? No, why?'

'Can we come in, please?'

'Of course.'

The officers entered. PC Leary immediately noticed the fake Crown Jewels on the coffee table. 'What's that?' he asked and pointed at her handiwork.

'School project,' Chloe said.

'You've put a lot of work into them,' PC Jacobs said kindly as he turned to take a closer look.

Chloe nodded. 'I've tried to make them just like the real thing!'

'Good job!'

'What's this about?' Edith asked.

PC Jacobs answered. 'We believe you can help us with our enquiries into the theft of the Crown Jewels—the real ones. We'd like you to come to the station with us.'

'That's ridiculous,' Edith said.

'I take it you don't mind me looking around?' PC Leary asked.

'Go ahead.'

A minute later, PC Leary emerged from Chloe and George's room with the replica Archie under his arm. He sat the teddy bear down on one of the sofas and sat next to him.

'What are you doing with my teddy bear?' Chloe asked, pretending to be annoyed.

George watched the blond officer suspiciously.

'There have been some unusual reports,' PC Jacobs said. 'People losing time. Some say they saw a bear matching your bear's description when it happened.'

Chloe frowned. 'He's just a toy.'

'But *is* he?' Leary asked. He turned to Archie. 'Archie, isn't it?'

The replica Archie sat there as a teddy bear would.

'He can't talk. He's a teddy bear,' Chloe said.

Leary ignored her and took out his cuffs. He cuffed Archie's paw to his own hand.

George sniggered, and PC Leary glared at him.

'Archie, I understand you're not what you seem,' Leary said.

'What exactly are you doing, officer?' Edith asked.

PC Jacobs covered his face with his hand.

Leary ignored Edith. 'It will be easier on your friends if you talk to me, Archie.'

Edith had to cover her mouth to suppress a laugh. Even Jacobs gave a gentle, embarrassed shake of his head.

Chloe snorted.

Leary turned. 'Quiet, please, or do I need to arrest you all? Don't think I won't do it.' He returned his attention to the toy bear. 'Archie, if you care about the people in this room, you will talk to me.'

Edith turned to the other officer. 'What's this about, really?'

'The Crown Jewels.' Jacobs said, looking somewhat awkward.

'Really?' Edith said, feigning awe. 'How exciting. And you think a teddy bear took them?'

PC Jacobs' radio crackled to life, and he put it to his mouth. 'Jacobs,' he said and, with a look of relief, walked into one of the bedrooms, out of earshot.

PC Leary flicked Archie in the face. There was no reaction.

'What are you expecting him to do?' Chloe asked. 'Bite you?'

'I know he can feel it,' snapped Leary.

Chloe crossed her arms. 'Yet you're still flicking him in the face? You're not very nice.'

Jacobs walked back into the room. 'The jewels are back. Someone used a drone to drop them at the Tower. Masters says to let them go.'

Leary stood up, holding the bear. It took him a moment to accept this news. 'Really?'

Jacobs nodded.

'Did they get the drone?'

'We sent our own drone after it, but we were too late.'

Chloe's eyes widened at this news.

Leary stepped onto the balcony and looked around. Moments later, he came back in. 'Look for a drone, or at least the controls.'

Jacobs nodded. 'Do you mind?' he asked Edith.

'Knock yourself out.'

The officers searched thoroughly but finally gave up. Leary had the replica Archie under his arm throughout. He reluctantly uncuffed the toy bear. 'That will be all for now.'

'Does this mean you're not arresting my daughter's teddy bear, officer?' Edith asked.

Leary regarded her coldly. 'That won't be necessary.'

PC Jacobs was a little friendlier. 'I'm sorry for the intrusion. We'll leave you in peace now.'

'Thank you, officer,' Edith said.

They let themselves out.

Edith waited until the officers' footsteps were far away and then winked at Chloe and George. She smiled.

Chloe started laughing.

George joined in, and finally, Edith couldn't help it. She looked at the replica Archie and burst into laughter.

CHAPTER 49

ARCHIE SURVIVED THE DRIVE back with the drone, and two days later, the control box also arrived at the house. With the drone and its controls back in the attic, it seemed to signify an end to their adventure. But it was not an end for Archie. After some initial jubilation at their success, things calmed down, and he was aware that Chloe, George, and Edith were talking about him. Sometimes he'd walk into the room, and they'd stop suddenly. And that was never a good sign.

He knew what was happening. Keeping him around presented a risk to them. The drone was back in the attic, but he was still there, and as long as that remained the case, he was a problem. They were probably right.

The family called him on Monday night after Chloe and George returned from school. This is it, Archie thought. He entered the kitchen to find Chloe, George, and Edith sitting at the long island.

'Hi,' Archie said and lumbered forward.

Chloe was struggling to sit still. 'We've got a present for you.'

Archie tried to smile. A leaving present, he thought to himself.

Chloe passed him a small box with a ribbon on it.

Archie accepted it. 'Thanks.' He undid the ribbon and gently opened the box. Inside was a key. He picked it up and looked at them.

Chloe smiled. 'We'd like you to live with us, Archie.'

'Live with you?'

'Of course, assuming you want to. What did you think we were going to say?'

'I thought you were going to ask me to leave.'

'Aww, Archie,' Edith said. 'Of course not!'

Chloe jumped down from her stool. 'We're your family now, Archie.' She ran up and hugged him. 'And this is your home.'

'Well, until we find our own place,' Edith said. 'But of course, you'll come with us unless you have other plans.'

Archie struggled to talk. He turned away for a second to gather his emotions. He turned back and gave a huge smile. 'Thank you. This is all I ever wanted.'

Edith wiped a tear from her eye. 'You're welcome.'

CHAPTER 50

DETECTIVE EDDIE MASTERS PUSHED a vacuum cleaner along his hallway towards the front room. Now and then, Roswell jumped at the device and took a swipe at it.

'Don't be so daft, Roswell!' He leaned down and ruffled the cat's fur. 'I'll play with you in a minute.'

Despite the cat, he made it into the front room and pulled the armchair out to get to the back. As he pushed the vacuum cleaner attachment behind the armchair, there was an unexpected sucking noise.

Masters withdrew the attachment and found a folded note stuck to the end. He opened it up and read:

We can't involve you any further. Please give us until the press conference to sort this out. Thank you for everything, E. x

Masters' mouth fell open. They hadn't deserted him—they just didn't want to involve him. He sat down and, after a moment, sent a brief text to Edith: *Just found your note behind the armchair. I thought the worst. Sorry. Eddie x*

He wondered why he'd put a kiss at the end, but it was too late now—the message was gone. Maybe he shouldn't have sent it at all. And why should he be sorry? Also, too late. He sighed, closed his eyes and made a mental note to re-read texts before sending them.

A few days passed. It was a beautiful morning, and Masters sat at the dining room table with his breakfast. He looked out of his rear window and watched a small bird peck at some nuts hanging in a net from a tree in his garden.

There was a clang as his letterbox rattled shut. Masters retrieved his mail. It was a quiet day—just the one letter. He opened it up.

You are invited to join Edith, Chloe, George and Archie for an evening of fine dining and conversation. Smart dress preferred. Hope to see you on Saturday 18th Jan at 7pm.

The next couple of days dragged by, and Masters couldn't help but reflect on what had happened. There was, of course, still an ongoing investigation into the theft of the jewels. The drone had been picked up on a few cameras, but it was too far off to make out any details, and, in any case, any distinguishing marks had been covered up. The photos taken at The Tower of London concentrated on the unusually decorated package it had been carrying, so they were of little use in identifying the drone. Authorities were not sure how it had vanished.

How the criminals had frozen time or people, walked past heavily-armed guards and then left with the priceless jewels was deemed a mystery. Some said aliens were responsible.

Stories of Londoners freezing after seeing a bear were put down to mass hysteria. No one had paid too much attention to the story. How could it be true?

It occurred to him that somewhere out there, someone would have clippings of events on a board similar to his own. But this time, there was one difference. He knew the truth.

Saturday arrived, and Masters had done as asked. He'd invested in a smart black jacket and crisp white shirt and now stood at Edith's door, ringing the bell.

As steps approached, he nervously held a bottle of champagne out.

Chloe opened the door. 'For me! You shouldn't have.'

Masters coughed and laughed. 'Hello Chloe, I was expecting your mum.'

'Come in.'

Masters walked down the hallway to find George, Edith, and Archie hanging out in the kitchen with the cooking. They were dressed in their hotel best. In the centre of the kitchen on the island were the fake jewels.

'Oh wow,' Masters said. 'These are excellent! Obviously, one of my colleagues saw these at the hotel, which explained my "mistake", so thank you. It really helped.'

Chloe beamed. 'I thought you'd like to see them.'

Masters' eyes settled on Archie.

Archie held a paw up. 'Yes, I'm real. You didn't imagine me.'

Masters grinned. 'I did wonder.' He showed the hair stuck to his wrist. 'I kept this just in case.'

Edith smiled. She seemed excited to see him. 'I'm glad you came. I wanted the chance to thank you properly.'

'It was kind of you to invite me. I'll admit, I'm curious to hear about your adventures after you left my house.'

'I'm so sorry,' Edith said. 'I know you trusted us, but it seemed wrong to involve you more than we already had.'

'I wanted to wait,' George said.

'Thank you, George.'

'But once we heard you were giving the press conference,' Edith continued. 'I mean, you're a police officer. We couldn't ask you to stand at a podium and lie to the whole country for us.'

'It wasn't ideal,' Masters agreed. 'If only I'd found that note sooner, it might have helped... well, possibly. Where did you put it?'

'The dining room table.'

'Hmm. I suspect Roswell's involvement here. Your drone decoration was interesting. Very clever, and you'll be happy to know that it worked. We have plenty of photos of stripey legs, but none of the drone of any use for identification.'

Edith smiled. 'I am a little relieved.'

'Well, congratulations. You will all make excellent criminals.'

The room went quiet.

Masters laughed. 'I'm joking. I'm assuming you're not planning any more heists, Archie?'

'Did you have anything in mind?' Archie asked.

'Most definitely not!'

'Are you okay, detective?' Edith asked. 'I would imagine you had some explaining to do?'

'Call me Eddie, please.' He scratched his head as he thought back. 'I think a few senior police officers found my actions suspicious, but in the end, they were just relieved to get the jewels back and wanted the story to go away. So yes, I'm okay. How about all of you?'

'I'm okay,' Chloe said. 'I made a new friend at school.'

'Glad to hear it!' Masters said with a smile. 'Probably best not to mention the Crown Jewels.'

'But it's my best story!' Chloe whined.

Masters gave her a mock stern look, and she laughed. 'And how are you, George?'

'I'm fine. Glad that normality has returned.' He looked at Archie. 'Well, almost.'

'You know you love me,' Archie responded.

George grimaced, but it was in good humour.

Masters looked at Edith.

'I'm good. Maybe I needed an adventure.' Edith jumped up, wrapped her arms around Masters, and then let him go. 'Thank you for not locking us all up. I'm so sorry we left you thinking the worst.'

Masters looked a little embarrassed. 'You're welcome.' He looked at the family and smiled. 'You work well together.'

'We do, don't we?' Edith looked proudly at Chloe and George.

Masters turned to Archie. 'So, Archie, what's the plan now? What are you going to do with yourself?'

Archie shrugged. 'It would be nice to know why I'm alive... but without some drastic surgery to see what's inside me, that may be difficult.'

'There are some sharp scissors in the draw,' George said.

Archie gasped in mock horror. 'You first.'

'Are they always like this?' Masters asked.

Edith laughed. 'Yep.'

'I'm not sure what to do,' Archie said. 'It's kind of difficult for me to get a job.'

'I can imagine.'

'Unless you need a deputy?'

'I'll keep it in mind.'

At that moment, Edith's mobile rang, and she answered.

'Carole! It's nice to hear from you... you're what...? Back early morning! Yes, that's a lovely surprise. I've got a few things to tell you when you're here....'

After a brief chat, Edith ended the call. She looked unsure of herself.

'Are you okay?' Masters asked.

'Yes, it will be lovely to see my sister.'

'I'm sensing a but....'

Edith smiled. 'Well, I've got some explaining to do....'

Masters waited. He knew there was more to come.

'...and she's such an overachiever,' Edith added guiltily. 'I can't help feeling like a bit of a failure around her.'

'Er, hello!' Chloe said indignantly and pointed at herself. 'You had me! You did great, Mum.'

Everyone laughed, even George.

THE END

ABOUT THE AUTHOR

Anthony is a British writer living in Worthing. He's a lifelong civil servant but hopes to put that behind him one day in favour of more enjoyable ways of financing the rent.

This is his first novel. And his first attempt at illustrating a novel, a process he enjoyed but wishes humans were more box-like—they'd be so much easier to draw.

He is currently planning a book for young adults called The Strange House of Albert Grand, in which a computer-obsessed teen and his tough younger sister discover clues that their grandfather may be an infamous inventor. Their enquiries lead them to a deadly subterranean world beneath his mansion.

To offer huge movie deals or anything else, you can contact me at: anthonyconradauthor@gmail.com

ACKNOWLEDGMENTS

I enlisted the help of several fabulous freelancers to complete this book. Thank you to my beta reader, Wordsprite, for her insightful feedback. A huge thank you to my editor, Rachel Le Mesurier, for her invaluable and patient assistance. All errors are entirely my own, and I've probably added a few more since then, just for good measure. Big thanks to Martina Delloca for the fantastic cover artwork. She's an incredible artist. (The interior drawings are my own efforts—sorry about that). Finally, thankyou to my family for their feedback and encouragement and for putting up with me waffling about sentient toy bears.

Printed in Great Britain
by Amazon

21363178R00142